Always Rember,
You are Braver
than you think
            Stronger
than you seem and
        Loved More
than you know!

Joyce Keating Steinert
Kevin Matus

NEVER UNDERESTIMATE THE STRENGTH OF WOMEN

N.U.S.W.

Created by Joyce Keating Steinert
and Kerin Martucci

NEVER UNDERESTIMATE THE STRENGTH OF WOMEN
Created by Joyce Keating Steinert and Kerin Martucci

Second Edition
Copyright©2016 by Joyce Keating Steinert and Kerin Martucci

ISBN 13: 9780692762295
LCCN: 2016913627

Cover modifications and interior Layout by Ellie Searl, Publishista®

Edited by Amanda Neal and Ellie Searl, Publishista®

Cover Photography by Christine Foster

Graphic Art by Nicki Stevenson

www.nustrengthofwomen.com

First Edition print version published in 2010

KAM Consultants, Inc.
West Chester, PA

CONTENTS

DEDICATION AND ACKNOWLEDGMENTS..*9*

INTRODUCTION BY JOYCE KEATING STEINERT....................................*15*

DR. AISHA BAILEY..*19*

ALICE CLEVELAND...*21*

AMELIA MORÁN CEJA...*25*

AMY BIELINSKI..*29*

ANISA ROMERO...*35*

ANNETTE M. SANCHEZ..*39*

BERNICESTINE MCLEOD BAILEY...*45*

CAROLE HOCHMAN...*53*

CHRISSY SPARROW..*57*

DAWN JUNEAU..*63*

DIANE LANG..*67*

DR. KATHLEEN HANDS..*71*

ELAINE GORDON...*81*

JEANNE BICE AND ANGEL SMEDLEY...*91*

ANGEL SMEDLEY...*97*

JILL HOLTERMANN BOWERS...*99*

JULIE DEFRUSCIO...*103*

LIZ LANGE...*109*

LORI DENNIS..*113*

LUCIA BURNS (AKA LUCIA RAMAZETTI ON YOUTUBE)..........................*117*

MELLODY HOBSON...*123*

NANCE L. SCHICK, ESQ....*125*

PAULETTE ROBINSON...*133*

SANDY STEIN...*139*

TERESA ALEXANDER...*143*

THE MISSION OF THIS BOOK..*147*

NEVER UNDERESTIMATE THE STRENGTH OF WOMEN is dedicated in memory of my beautiful beloved little sister Rita Karen Reynolds, who lost her life trying to save another. Her strength and courage lives on!

DEDICATION AND ACKNOWLEDGMENTS

FROM JOYCE KEATING STEINERT

To MY DAUGHTER KERIN - *there are no words for your specialness; you have my heart!*

To Suzanne *–what special gifts you possess; you have my heart!*

To My:

Loving Sister, Brother, and Sister-in-law – Peggy, Bernard, and Eileen

Bonus Sons - Bruce and Gary

Nieces - Amanda, Denise, Eileen, Melissa, Renee, and Tara

Nephews - Adam, Doug, Evan, Jerry, Patrick, Paul, Timothy, and Walter Jr.

–The world is a better place because you're in it!

To George Coyne *–thank you for being you and for your generosity and trust.*

To Dr. Jack Schwartz, Dr. Romeo Caballes, Marilyn DiBlasi Spano, Leslie Heman Steinert, Bonnie Lynn Hall, Shirlee Richards Colanduoni, and Krissy Flynn *–you're dear to my heart.*

To Great Supporter, Ellie Searl, Publishista and all the remarkable talented women who said "yes" to N.U.S.W. *–no words express how grateful and blessed we feel.*

To My Heroes: Hillary Rodham Clinton, Eleanor Roosevelt, Oprah Winfrey, and Ellen DeGeneres *–your strength, courage, tenacity, and leadership guide all women*

To my Courageous Great Grandmother Elizabeth Clouer, a tenacious entrepreneur and owner of The Inn, Rockaway Queens *–sorry I never met you.*

FROM KERIN MARTUCCI

———◆———

T O MY MOM: "You are my ambassador of Quan."[1]
I would like to say a special thank you for the following people in my life:

M. St. John. If it wasn't for M. this book would have never gotten off the ground. She believed in me and this book. Her words were simply, "Go and make it happen Bella!" Thank you.

To my dearest Aunt Leslie Heman Steinert, if it wasn't for her my childhood would've been bleak! All of my memories going to Aunt Leslie's were filled with love. Aunt Leslie's house was my "Alice in Wonderland," the brooks, streams, gardens, ponds, stone bridges, bunnies and sweet honeysuckle vines. They were the best times of my life; every child should grow up with an Aunt Leslie, in an environment filled with such beauty and innocence. She taught me to appreciate the outdoors and to tap into my creativity. Her Grandfather, Wilhelm Hermann willed my aunt the house in this bucolic setting for a reason…he knew Aunt Leslie would appreciate and fulfill his vision, for she embodies the grace and beauty of his enchanted homeland of Germany. Thank you for including me into your family, summers with Uncle Roger, Missy (my partner in crime), Amanda, and Evan, I will cherish these memories always! My bonus brothers Gary and Bruce, you have my heart.

To my father, Robert Martucci, "Faccia Bella." Our time was too short . . . Your daughter always.

My deceased "GrandMaMa" Connie Martucci; thank you for teaching me at the age of seven about hard work and good business ethics. On my weekend visits with my father Robbie I would spend time with my GrandMaMa, as she liked to be called. My GrandMaMa was a true entrepreneur. She was the Regional Sales Manager for Stanley Home Products and later opened her own candy store simply called "Connie's" in Staten Island, New York.

Sunday mornings we would wake at 4 a.m. to pick up the Sunday

---

[1] from *Jerry McGuire*

papers and place them in the back of her Vega, where we would have to put the inserts in the papers before the store opened at 7 a.m. She taught me two things: the customer is always right and the value of making a dollar. She was a hard worker, but never complained. A motto GrandMaMa always lived by was: "Have your hair and nails done, never leave the house without make-up on and lip gloss." I never knew how much money she made. She had a very generous nature, and supported the people who came into their store who were down on their luck. She never let anyone know…but I did! She was a true Sagittarian, a people person, and knew all of her customers by their first names. Although she could stand up for herself, she often wore her heart on her sleeve. I believe she had the gene that allowed her to "sell ice to Eskimos!" She had a great gift of gab, and could sell anything. Thank you, GrandMaMa, you're truly the "Spirit" of this book and for that I am blessed to have had you for my Grandmother!

Nanny Reynolds, who is deceased, also owned a part of my heart. Rita Quinn Keating Reynolds was my Nanny, as she liked to be called. Nanny was a kind, gentle and feisty woman all rolled into one. My mother shared with me that when I was born, I truly saved my Nanny's life. Nanny lived a very challenging life; she had endured so much loss and tragedy at an early age. But when she buried her beautiful 8-year-old daughter RitaKaren after a horrific drowning (she died trying to save another child) my mother Joyce didn't know if her mother would make it through another day…I was born one year after my aunt died, so my Nanny's focus was on the baby…me! My Nanny would tell me wonderful stories of her growing up in Larchmont, New York and summers in her beloved "Hudson River." Nanny was always so loving and funny with me. I never really saw her cry, but even as a small child I knew behind her jokes and laughter she hid her pain well. Nanny did the best she could with the hand she was dealt. She threw all her love, wisdom and advice into me. My mom said I saved her, but really she did the same for me! I love you Nanny and I hope you're looking down on me and Mom with those smiling Irish eyes!

To my QVC girls:

I wanted to acknowledge the women that I have been privileged to work with for over 20 years. They are moms, single moms, business owners, doctors, lawyers, nurses, weather anchors, actresses and forging entrepreneurs.

They have all inspired me to create this book, and I am proud to call them all my friends. The times we have shared, through laughter and tears, the break-ups, weddings, graduations, births and even deaths.

What their support and friendship has bestowed on my life is truly priceless! QVC might have given me a job, but I am the one who is lucky to experience the lifelong friendships with these amazing women.

To all my friends who are truly beautiful inside and out, thank you for touching my life and giving me strength, love, support and sisterhood. I celebrate you, and I am a better person for knowing you all! Thank you!

My own heroes are Amelia Earhart, Jacqueline Kennedy, Jane Austen and Sandra Bullock. These women have demonstrated great strength, grace and calm as they forged forward in the face of adversity.

My words of wisdom come from the brilliant poet George Bernard Shaw: "Progress is impossible without change, and those who cannot change their minds cannot change anything."

INTRODUCTION BY JOYCE KEATING STEINERT

IT WAS UPON THE COMPLETION of my first book which dealt with five generations of women in our family, that I was so proud to learn the strength of my Great Grandmother Elizabeth Clouer, along with her sisters became successful hotel entrepreneurs. It was Kerin's suggestion that we explore today's women entrepreneurs. Kerin simply stated, "Mom, I am so fortunate to work with remarkable women entrepreneurs. Their stories are amazing and inspirational. Let me ask, all they can say is 'no'." Well they didn't say "NO," they all believed in us and what we are trying to accomplish. The premise of the book is simple—we want to reach girls at risk before they fall through the cracks. I want all girls/women to pick up this book and be inspired when they read about women from all walks of life, the journey and roads they traveled and how they handled the bumps along the way. We will be the shoulders they stand upon!

NEVER UNDERESTIMATE THE STRENGTH OF WOMEN takes on the important role of lighting up that "neon sign" and calling all women to empower themselves.

The following are remarkable, awe-inspiring journeys filled with grace, intelligence, courage, tenacity and the common thread of strength.

I thought it important during this time of great idealism, while adolescent girls are actively searching for meaning, that we keep the safety net up and respect their uniqueness and encourage their growth into productive adults. "NUSW" is one of those nets. This book is all about empowerment. How fortunate are we that these remarkable women share their knowledge, spirit, and incredible strength through their personal experiences and by giving young girls the words of wisdom and heroic inspirations that have helped them along the way!

NEVER UNDERESTIMATE THE STRENGTH OF WOMEN is a page turner. You will actually feel as though you're walking right along with these women, holding their hands through doors that state: "Enter at your own risk."

photo by Harold Bailey, Jr.Aisha Bailey

DR. AISHA BAILEY

D R. AISHA BAILEY IS THE CEO of Aisha & Co. LLC, a toy/gift/stationery manufacturing company. In addition, she is currently on staff at the K. Hovnanian Hospital of The Jersey Shore University Medical Center in Neptune, New Jersey as a resident physician in pediatrics. Dr. Bailey founded Aisha & Co. and her signature product line Ishababies in 2004. As a pediatrician, Dr. Bailey saw the beauty in all children and wanted all children to see and respect the beauty in all people.

Dr. Bailey is a graduate of Phillips Exeter Academy and a member of Brown University's graduating class of 1999 with an AB in English— fulfilling her lifelong commitment to writing. In 2009, she attained her medical degree with honors from the University of Medicine and Dentistry of New Jersey's School of Osteopathic Medicine (UMDNJ-SOM) in Stratford, New Jersey. She is certified by the Board of Osteopathic Medical Examiners. Prior to medical school attendance, Dr.

Bailey served as an assistant to the New York City Deputy Medical Examiner during the identification process of victims of the World Trade Center and Flight 587 tragedies in the role of family liaison. In addition, she did research on two projects at Columbia Presbyterian Hospital in New York; one related to hypertension studies involving DNA and the other related to the efficiency of admissions rates of pediatric patients in the emergency room.

While attending UMDNJ, Dr. Bailey did research on Human papillomavirus (HPV) at Monmouth Medical Center in Monmouth, New Jersey where she subsequently developed cervical cancer education materials in English and Spanish, and presented her findings at a conference of the American College of Obstetricians and Gynecologists. She also served in several leadership roles in professional organizations while at UMDNJ, including Treasurer of her school's local chapter of the Student National Medical Association (SNMA) the year they won the SNMA Chapter of the Year Award, the school's liaison and representative to the Undergraduate American Association of Osteopathy (UAAO) and a nationally elected officer (National Coordinator) serving on the National Executive Board of the UAAO with responsibility for communications among all of the UAAO member schools. She currently belongs to the American Osteopathic Association and the American College of Osteopathic Pediatricians.

In starting Aisha & Co. and in launching the trademarked Ishababies line, Dr. Bailey has combined her passion for medicine with her passion for design. She currently holds four design patents for her characters with more in process and has received the following awards and recognition: Seal of Excellence from *Creative Child Magazine*, two nominations for Best New Product at the National Stationery Show, and the appearance of two of her characters on the April 2009 cover of *Playthings* magazine. She and her acclaimed Ishababies have been featured in the *University Medicine Magazine* of UMDNJ, the *Courier Post* of South Jersey, CBS's *The Early Show*, Toy Fair TV, editorial coverage in *Giftware News* and *The Westport News* among other publications. Ishababies is sold in over 200 gift and toy specialty stores across the United States, Canada, UK, Bermuda, Aruba, Mexico, Saudi Arabia and San Maarten. Ishababies are designed to be pancultural, appealing to all people across all segments. They are baby-safe, fully washable, and have luxuriously soft cotton exteriors complemented by internal filling of all new material.

Dr. Bailey continues to be committed at all times to ensuring that all children have the opportunity to enjoy Ishababies. To that end, Aisha & Co. has made sizeable gifts of Ishababies to children through Toys for Tots (in part contributed to children affected by Hurricane Katrina) and to foster children who participate in the NJ Cares program housed at UMDNJ-SOM.

———◆———

I was born in Boston, Massachusetts. One of my earliest memories was asking Buckminster Fuller "How do you make things?" when I was in kindergarten at Milton Academy. I then moved with my family to Dallas, Texas and subsequently came to reside in Westport, Connecticut. Growing up, our family vacations were walking, climbing and riding adventures to unusual places that showed us how people from other backgrounds and environments lived and adapted to their environments.

When I was 12, my family travelled to Alaska and saw many polar and grizzly bears, caribou, arctic foxes and bearded seals. We hiked Denali National Park & Preserve's mountains and glaciers. I also fondly remember walking across Hawaii's volcanoes and varied landscapes on our many vacations to Hawaii.

Sports became an early fascination for me and I spent most of my time playing organized soccer and basketball throughout my childhood. At the age of 13, I was selected to play for Connecticut's Olympic development team as a goalkeeper and continued to pursue my love of soccer, basketball and track throughout high school. I began attending Phillips Exeter Academy in my junior year and was elected a proctor in my dorm during senior year in addition to being a triple varsity athlete.

As a Brown undergraduate, staying with families in Zimbabwe and assisting at AIDS clinics, I worked with a very special physician who nursed villagers back to health using the few tools that he had available to him, along with love and respect for his patients. Later, I lived in the

Amazon rain forests of Venezuela with the Yekuana Indians, studying their traditions and medicine.

After 9/11, I assisted the Deputy Director of the WTC investigations and was a family liaison for victims of the World Trade Center disaster. I came to realize how important and healing it is to connect with those who have been devastated by serious loss or illness. In 1998 and 1999, I worked with pediatric patients at the Hasbro Children's Hospital in Providence. As Co-Coordinator of Playroom Activities, I helped the children express their internalized emotions through play, reading and art.

I have always been blessed with a strong sense of self and purpose. I remember roaming around my yard as a girl, finding shapes in the clouds and creating my own world. I know that I dreamed about being a girl who could do anything—since this is what my parents told me at every opportunity. I know that I emulated both of them, but I especially looked up to my mother as an example of what a woman should be. Though it was very painful to be dropped off at day care and say goodbye to a sometimes tearful mother, I learned that mommies worked. This experience helped me to dream about being a woman who could be a police officer, a firefighter, a doctor…it was up to me.

When I was four, my mother quit her job to start her own consulting company. This was at a time when it was still pretty taboo for women to work, much less start a company. I remember watching my mother juggle work, soccer practice, karate, basketball games, track meets, cooking dinner, washing clothes, heading up civic organizations, being active in her alma mater and still having time to catch her breath… occasionally. Her creativity and versatility was extremely important to me and I know that without her, I would have had a *very* small number of dreams.

My maternal grandfather was one of the most extraordinary people that I have ever met. He was a devoted husband and father, a college graduate, a deacon in his church and a dedicated postal worker for over 25 years. Most importantly, he was a man of his word who led by example. My grandfather was a man equipped with compassion, a friend who others turned to for help and sometimes a shoulder to cry on. He was a man who made people want to do their personal best when he was around. I believe this was because my grandfather really *saw* people—about who they were spiritually and understood that this life was truly about spiritual evolution.

I remember spending summers with my grandparents and sitting with my grandfather while he tended to his garden with care, and watching him cook dinner for the family and bake his famous banana pudding from scratch. Sometimes, I would go on errands with Granddaddy and he would take food to ill parishioners, or shuttle church members to the store or wherever they needed to go. Granddaddy rarely raised his voice; his presence cast a strange inner calm among those whose lives he touched. He was a man who believed in hard work, but knew that the real hard work was dealing with the spiritual struggles that people encounter every day.

I truly believe that my grandfather was integral in my spiritual foundation. He showed me what it was to be a truly great person. I still follow much of what he taught me and most of what I do is because of him and his legacy. Through his example I gained a more positive view of the world and a solid value system that has been my "spiritual compass" and foundation. These values are: (1) To love God and family (2) To treat others with respect while being compassionate and discerning (3) To really *see* all people for who they are and who they are trying to become since we are all evolving in life's never ending journey (4) To have honor and integrity in everything that I do.

I keep seeing so many girls growing up now who are lost and have little or no self-esteem. It seems even harder to exist in this world now, especially if you are different from others. *But, the truth is that everyone is different because they were meant to be.* We *all* have various jobs to do on earth and need to celebrate that. I have always been different from other people. But it was this difference that helped me to see the world in special ways and still helps me to keep creating and thriving. My uniqueness is my lifeline. It is what inspires me day after day and helps me think of new ways to solve old problems. It is this state of mind that helps me constantly achieve.

Don't be afraid of success. Whether in class or in life, don't be afraid to break new boundaries or to do well. There is no need to hold yourself back or undermine your God given gifts so that others can feel better about themselves. This is especially true of the groups of people with which you surround yourself.

Please choose your friends wisely and make sure that you only surround yourself with people who make you feel better about yourself more than they make you feel bad. Choose individuals who you are able to speak with honestly and openly and people who are able to reciprocate this with you. Friendship should be a give and take. Don't keep people around who fill you with negative energy or stomp on your hopes and dreams. They are *not* your friends.

Don't be afraid to stand up for what you believe in. Sometimes you may have to do things alone, but do not be afraid of this. Gaining acceptance is fine, but gaining respect is extraordinary, no matter what others may tell you.

Finally, *never* ever give up on your dreams. Don't let others tell you what you are destined for...this really only depends on you and what you feel and know in your heart. As a little girl, I told everyone who I met growing up that I was going to be a doctor. As I went through school, I realized that I loved to write short stories and draw cartoon characters from my imagination. So, I decided to major in English Literature and start my own gift company, but that dream of being a doctor never went away. This dream kept me going through all the late-night study sessions and the many trials that I had to endure. But by the time I had formed my company *and* had gotten into medical school, I was tired. It was in talking to my family and friends that I realized that I could accomplish all things. I could be a doctor *and* still cultivate my artistic talents and my love for business.

Learn to embrace and love *all* aspects of yourself. Though they may not be in synch with one another, cultivate each talent and let all of your senses shine. Love yourself for who you are, love your imperfections—even if no one else does. You are your own worst critic, but you should *always* be your own best friend.

Dr. Aisha Bailey
Capital Pediatrics
2623 Centennial Blvd - Suite 103
Tallahassee, FL 32308
850-877-6119

ALICE CLEVELAND

ALICE CLEVELAND'S COMPANY IS TV Products International (TPI). The business offers a service to companies and vendors wishing to have their products marketed to television/electronic retailers, commonly referred to as "outlets." TPI acts as an exclusive agent to market and sell specific products for placement with these outlets. Outlets are the channels of distribution and territory for TPI's services which include television home shopping programming, predominately QVC, Home Shopping Network (HSN), Shop at Home, QVC London and Germany, ShopNBC and Worldwide Shopping Source (WSS) as well as infomercials and television spots.

As an independent contractor, Alice also works as a spokesperson/talent for specific companies and/or products mainly on QVC but also in television spots and infomercials.

I was born in Florida, and spent a large portion of my childhood growing up in the hills of eastern Kentucky. We lived in a very repressed coal mining town, where everyone was poor. It wasn't until we moved back to Florida that I realized just how poor we really were. We lived in government "projects." I can remember having pancakes for Thanksgiving dinner. There was no turkey or dressing, no pumpkin pie. Just the simple pancakes with syrup made from sugar and water to pour on top.

At a very early age I knew that I would be successful one day. I knew I didn't want to be poor for the rest of my life. It wasn't particularly profound, it was just a fact. I remember seeing *American Bandstand* with Dick Clark on my aunt and uncle's black and white television set. His job looked pretty easy to me, and I thought maybe I would do something like that when I grew up. I was always very personable. Mom said I never met a stranger, and I soon realized communications skills were a very big asset! It was easy to talk to people. I genuinely liked everyone, so being friendly and interested in others was natural for me. Years later, I had the pleasure of working alongside of Dick Clark. From the images in our minds to reality is really not that long of a trip.

Growing up I was a very homely child. My own grandmother used to comment, "It's good that Alice has such a sweet disposition because she is such a homely child." She also used to tell me that "pretty is as pretty does…so what if you're not pretty, you have a very pretty disposition." People would comment on how pretty my two sisters were and then turn to me and ask, "And whose child is this?" Obviously thinking, "My, what an ugly little girl." In retrospect, it was fine not being the "pretty one" because my personality was able to develop. I am who I am today because of everything I went through as a child. I was even paralyzed when I was young, only to overcome it and learn to walk again at the age of four. However, my large motor movements were a little delayed. I failed skipping in kindergarten.

Recounting all of this, it all really just comes down to attitude. I truly believe we all have choices. We are not all created equal. We don't all have the same opportunities, but we all have choices we make. I made a conscious choice to be successful. It didn't just happen. I've been fortunate to have been at the right place at the right time. But I put myself in those places. We cannot just sit and wait for our ship to come in, we must send out the fleet!

Growing up my heroes were my parents. My dad only had a sixth grade education but he was one of the smartest people I ever knew. It was not uncommon for my dad to read a couple of books a day! Both he and my mom always told us we could do anything we put our minds to.

My admiration and respect for both of my parents was (and is) tremendous. From the age of two until she was 16 my mom was raised in a Catholic orphanage. She married my dad when she was only 17 and he had just turned 18 years old. They were married for 46 years before cancer took Dad from us. Mom had to overcome a lot of adversities in her life. The feeling of abandonment was always present. She has suffered with severe depression all of her life, yet she did her best to raise my sisters and I with confidence and security.

I can remember singing the song "Let the Sun Shine In" when I was only in kindergarten. My dad taught me this song before I can remember. I would sing to myself: "Let the sun shine in. Face it with a grin. Frowners never win, smilers always do. So open up your heart and let the sun shine in" when I was trying to achieve anything in school, from winning at bingo to winning a spelling bee. I just kept on smiling…I just knew I'd win! Those lyrics spoke to me. It was about attitude. Of course, at that age I didn't even know what an attitude was, but I knew if I smiled and I didn't get mad about losing a game or a contest, that I would win the next time.

Today, if I could give only one gift to all the young people in the world it would be the gift of a "good attitude." We can't change things that will happen to us in life, but we certainly can change our attitude. I was molested as a child by an uncle and a cousin. I was "dirt poor" and made fun of at school. Some girls wouldn't be my friend because I didn't have nice new clothes or the latest hair cut. Only we have control of our attitude. I have several mottos I've lived by:

The Golden Rule: "Do unto others as you would have them do unto you." You cannot go wrong if you just put yourself in someone else's shoes.

Matthew 19:19: "Love thy neighbor as thy self...and honor thy Mother and Father."

From my grandmother on my dad's side: "Bloom where you are potted. "Sometimes we don't have control over where we have to be, especially as a child or young person, but we can "bloom" wherever life places us. It is up to us.

And, finally, a very simple little saying. It only has 10 words and none of the words are longer than two letters: "If it is to be, it is up to me!"

I think we need more than ever for young people to know they have the power within themselves to accomplish anything they desire. It is not true that we are all created equal. Some people are richer, some people are prettier, some people are smarter, but there is no one exactly like you. And no matter what your abilities are you can always achieve what you can dream!

photo by Norma Quintana Amelia Morán Ceja

AMELIA MORÁN CEJA

CEJA VINEYARDS WAS FOUNDED IN 1999, making Amelia Ceja the first Mexican-American woman elected President of a wine production company in the history of the wine industry. *Inc.* magazine selected Ceja Entrepreneur of the Year 2004 (one of seven) in the January 2005 issue. In addition, Ceja Vineyards was named Best New Winery in 2002 by over 90 of the world's most prestigious wine writers. As case production increased from 750 cases to 10,000 cases per year, Ceja wines has received numerous awards and extensive media coverage. Now, Ceja wines are offered at some of the most acclaimed restaurants in the United States such as French Laundry, The Carnelian Room, Mustards Grill, Madre's, Scala's Bistro, Gotham Bar and Grill, Le Cirque, Charlie Trotter's and Frontera Grill.

Ceja's contributions to the wine industry were recognized on March 15, 2005, when she was named Woman of the Year by the California

Legislature. "Amelia is a great role model for the next generation of Latinos," said Senator Wesley Chesbro. "She has not only broken the glass ceiling in a very competitive business but has earned respect throughout the wine industry." Ceja Vineyards continues to receive numerous awards and accolades, including being named one of the Ten Hottest Small Brands of 2007 in the United States by *Wine Business Monthly*, features in *Condé Nast Traveler* magazine and *The Best of Napa & Sonoma* magazine and an appearance on CNN's *Headline News.*

Salud! Napa—Taste the Lifestyle, a bicultural online cooking show, will debut in June 2010, and Amelia will be the hostess.

I was born in Las Flores, Jalisco, Mexico—an agricultural village with a population of 50 residents. My mother, my sister and I lived with my grandparents while my father worked in the United States. My grandmother, Josefa Fuentes, was a fabulous cook, and almost all the ingredients she used to prepare our meals came from her farm.

My grandmother raised chickens, cows, goats and pigs. My grandfather grew corn, beans and vegetables in his 20-hectare farm, and various wild greens and mushrooms flourished there.

The yearly supply of beans and corn for tortillas was selected after harvest and stored in an adobe room, and vegetables were harvested as needed. Cheese was made from both cows' and goats' milk and meat was readily available from my grandmother's animals.

My earliest memories are of helping Mamá Chepa, my maternal grandmother, in her kitchen, and being involved with her cooking. I stirred, cut, fetched and ultimately, at the age of eight, began my solo cooking career—I made a nopales (cacti) and potatoes mole for my friends. My playground became the kitchen and my grandmother's beautiful yard was where my very primitive make-believe restaurant existed. There, I explored flavors, textures and various food combinations. It was great fun.

I left my idyllic village at 12, when my father brought my mother, my sister and me to the Napa Valley. There, I was introduced to the whole process of winegrowing from the ground up, and to new ingredients of world cuisine. My interest in cooking intensified.

At 14, when I graduated from junior high school, my parents invited me to return to Mexico for high school, and I accepted. I went to an all-girls' preparatory school in Aguascalientes—one of Mexico's most beautiful colonial cities. At La Paz, the boarding school, nuns prepared the residents' meals, and the food was exquisite. I had the chance to delve even deeper into the world's most sophisticated cuisine: Mexican food! I also had the opportunity to travel throughout Mexico during my stay, where I discovered the richness and diversity of regional cuisine.

I returned to California at 16 and finished high school at Justin Siena in the city of Napa. I went to UC San Diego and majored in History and Literature. Once again, I began cooking for my friends and exploring the relationship between food and wine. Also, during college, I worked at wonderful restaurants and my knowledge of cooking increased.

Pedro and I were married in 1980, and soon after, together with his parents and his brother, Armando Ceja, we purchased our first parcel in our beloved Carneros. In the meantime, Armando was studying enology at UC Davis and working at Domaine Chandon. Finally, in 1986, we developed our first vineyard and planted Pinot Noir. Since we had been making wine with Armando since 1983, our philosophy in winemaking was evident from the get go: to produce wine that reflected the place where the fruit was grown, our farming practices and our gentle approach in the vinification process. Most importantly, the wine had to complement all the food that we love, and therefore, balance in our wine was central.

Since the Culinary Institute of America at Greystone opened in 1995, in St. Helena, I began taking week-long classes there. I've explored Mexican, Asian, French, Middle Eastern and Mediterranean cuisines with some of the most renowned chefs in the world. And, after Copia (the American Center for Wine, Food and the Arts) opened in downtown Napa in 2001, I continued my culinary education by attending seminars hosted by prestigious restaurants.

Ceja Vineyards was founded in 1999, and in 2001 we released our first commercial vintages which reflected the same seamless continuity of our previous non-commercial vintages. Our emphasis is in wine and food as a daily experience with family and friends—in creating beautiful memories with all the people that touch our lives.

A testament to the quality, beauty, and balance of our wines is readily visible in the wonderful restaurants that carry our Ceja wines throughout the United States ranging from French, Asian, and of course, Mexican food—We Are the New American Table. ¡Salud!

My heroines when I was growing up in Mexico were my mother and my grandmother. Their devotion and unconditional love nurtured my body and soul. I arrived in the Napa Valley in 1967, and soon after, I had the great privilege of meeting Cesar Chavez through my father who worked in a vineyard management company. Cesar's humility and his dedication to farm workers' rights shaped my philosophy in life and in business: always be fair.

Words of wisdom to young girls: education, education, education, education. It gives you mobility everywhere. You have convictions; trust them and follow them. Find a mentor that you admire and respect.

wine@cejavineyards.com

707-255-3954

AMY BIELINSKI

AMY BIELINSKI'S STORY PROVES THAT even when life is physically, emotionally and spiritually challenging, personal strength and generosity to others can triumph.

It was the fall of 2009 and Amy was still recuperating from a serious stroke, but she found the time to think of others. On the local news she heard about a little boy who was suffering extensive brain damage after being hit by a car and how the family was struggling. As Amy quickly remembered how her church, family, friends and neighbors pulled through for her during her own medical crisis, she knew this was a call for her to give back. She went to all the retail stores on suburban Philadelphia's Main Line area for food and clothing and everyone gave so generously. Only one major chain declined; Amy doesn't shop there anymore. Several anonymous monetary donations were also made, as well as from lots of people who Amy shared the story with.

She packed her four children (all under the age of 10) into their SUV. They had loaded it up the night before, and all her children picked a gift of their own to give as well. They pulled up into the driveway to a house badly in need of repair, and filled the front porch with all the presents. All the children were so excited, but stayed extra quiet. As they drove away they started to sing Christmas songs. Realizing they had all learned a wonderful lesson, and hearing not one complaint, Amy was truly proud of her children. To this day, the family doesn't know who their Guardian Angel was!

After experiencing several weeks of severe neck pain, I drove myself to the emergency room at 5 a.m., steering with only my left hand, with all of my family still sleeping. My intuition was strong that there was something seriously wrong. I was sent home with pain medications and an appointment for an MRI the next day, which showed an artery dissection and a lack of blood flowing to my brain causing the neurological episodes. Rushed to a downtown hospital, I awaited the unknown.

Struggling with nausea, dizziness, confusion and unsteady balance, my husband and I left the MRI and rushed to critical care in a downtown hospital where I awaited my fate. No more relief from the pain, I sat with my husband wide-eyed praying the dissection had ceased. Finally came the news: "We don't know what caused it or if the pain is telling us the tear is continuing. We believe you've had a stroke and your arm and walking/balance will need intensive rehab to regain movement." Terror and fear flowed through every cell in my body. I prayed and pleaded and said a million I love yous to my family.

I stared blankly at my husband, and felt my whole life flash before me. I watched him move and carry himself in that small room in a way I had never witnessed. The life I had been blessed with had been such a gift. During the onset of the dissection, I made a phone call to say goodbye to my sister. I begged her to move on, to not miss me or feel sad. I didn't want to worry about her from heaven. She begged me to fight, to breathe and to pray.

I fought with all the might I had, only to realize its futility. What would be was not in our hands. Not mine, not my mother's, not my four young children who need their mom. Once I gave up that fight I felt free…peace like never before.

Much later, grateful for all the generous help from friends, family, and the Bryn Mawr Rehabilitation Hospital, I wrote them all the following letter:

I could never put into words my sincere gratitude and humble thankfulness. Your generous support has been overwhelming to our family. I would like to share a portion of this experience, as I never want to forget just how fortunate I am.

There was a day, several hours I suppose, when I felt the raw reality of what was wrong, and that I had no control over it. In that time there of course was fear and such a sense of despair. Every inch of my soul was so scared.

A strip, almost like film of an old movie, played in my mind. It was full of sheer happiness and love. People were popping into the picture from various times in my life, smiling, engaging in conversation and laughing. The strip ended with an aerial view of my children playing in the driveway and my mom at the front door holding baby Wade. She was smiling and waving emphatically…was she waving goodbye to me?

I wanted to ask, "Why?" So young and so much to leave. This thought went in and out of my head so quickly. What was meant to be would be. I wanted to be sure my loved ones didn't mourn if I left this world. They would simply miss me as I would miss them, and one day we would meet again.

I was unable to use my right arm, and I soon became unable to walk. Being transferred to Bryn Mawr Rehab was the most amazing ride I will ever take. It was a busy day in the city as I was preparing to leave Jefferson Hospital. Men in suits quickly walking and talking on their cell phones, mothers walking their babies and an older man selling flowers. I wanted to say, "Slow down, enjoy this day, look at this beautiful sky and the trees, it is so gorgeous...do you know how lucky we are? Be kind. That man in the suit— say hello to that sweet man selling flowers. Hug and love that baby. Try to make someone's day a little brighter. This we have control over. Our health, our time here...no. That is up to God."

I had a beautiful view as we moved along an unusually empty highway. I watched as Dave's car drove closely behind. I reflected on everything. Have I told Dave enough what an amazing father I think he is? Just behind Dave a car was passing. I noticed the shine of the grey metallic and the shape as it got closer to my back windows. It then sped on, as it should, it was passing us. It was a hearse. A beautiful, shiny, grey hearse. It moved on, as my husband said later, it went out of sight. Who was driving that hearse? Was it meant for me to see? Tears rolled down my face as I realized I was meant to live.

The first few weeks were trying, yet I was so thankful to be here. I was able to hug my children every day, and smell that sweet smell of a baby. I had the greatest of therapists and the greatest of friends and family. All of which I could not have done without.

This story is something I will carry forever. The despair, gratitude and love are emotions I will never forget. A sense of normalcy is finally in our home; I just try to hug and love more. And realize just how lucky I am.

I want all of you to know how thankful I am to each of you. You all in your own way have touched my life in a way I will never forget. I felt like I was being "carried" by this amazing group. We are so lucky to have this community and each other to pull us through...even in the most unexpected of times.

Much love and cheers the happiest of 2008 Amy Bielinski

My hero is my sister Ginny who is seven years older. Anything that I have gone through in life (good or bad) she has been there as my biggest supporter and voice of reason. When I'm in doubt of my actions, she has been the mother hen. We shared in each other's accomplishments but she has done more for me by far than I could ever begin to repay. She protected me from the magnitude and devastation of my husband's open heart surgery, counseled me as I questioned just where my place here was in this big world and when friends let me down she was the best person to dish it to.

When I had the stroke, I worried about my husband and the four small children we were raising. We had a home, mortgage, schedules…this crazy life that we could hardly come up for air from. It was in the plan for me to be pulled from this…temporarily. I cried for my children, husband and for my mom who I could hardly stand to see because the pain she felt for me was so intense. My sister, my hero, showed up every morning at 6 a.m. with my sweet 5-month-old baby in one hand and in the other, a holder with two steaming cups of Dunkin' Donuts coffee. We were extra quiet as we sipped our coffee and talked of the plan for each day.

Her life was put on hold. Nothing was about her. She and my other siblings took over the schedules, bills, laundry, homework…and she was there for every single therapy session. She had her notebook with her, always charting my progress and writing questions about my therapy. Always encouraging me. The fourth day of therapy I seemed to be doing worse. I had no sense of balance; I couldn't walk and had no use of my arm. The therapist told me to put fruit in a bowl with my good hand. Through the mirror I saw Ginny's hands covering her face as she cried, saying "I'm sorry, I don't want to see her like this…it is so bad." I laughed and reminded her where we were…lucky to be right here right now. So what if I can never walk or use my arm? I get to see you, and everyone else. I can love, cry, laugh…I can live. This is a gift.

I would remind young people, "this too shall pass." I remember using this phrase of my father's in times of great sadness. In life there are so many times you fall, or don't meet someone's expectations… sometimes even your own. Let's be gentle and kind to ourselves and realize if we had a magic ball to change something we would never grow to be who we are!

photo by Shelli Hyrkas

ANISA ROMERO

ANISA ROMERO ART & DESIGN is an interior design and art business. She believes that how you live and what you surround yourself with affects daily as well as spiritual life. Anisa is inspired by a holistic approach to interior design and believes a design should reflect a client's aesthetic, interests and needs. She aims for all aspects of a design to be innovative, artistic and beneficial—not only for the person living in or using the space—but for the environments as well. Organization is paramount. It is the key to an uncluttered life and mind. Everything in perfect rhythm.

Anisa Romero is a LEED AP, has her MA in Painting form New York University and an associate's degree in Interior Architecture from Parsons School of Design.

I grew up in the Northwest. I was a tumultuous teenager and was not content with the status quo. I was fortunate enough to be accepted as Rotary exchange student and went to live abroad in Brazil my junior year of high school. This was such an amazing opportunity for a small town girl. It really demonstrated the complexities of the world around me and allowed me to step out of my known universe of high school trivialities.

My challenging teenage years only got more so when I returned from my year abroad. In my last month of high school I was diagnosed with Hodgkin's disease, a lymphatic cancer. I spent the summer of 1986 and my first year of college at the University of Washington in treatment. This event really shifted the course of my life. It gave me the opportunity to not dwindle away my time and to really live in the present. I remember enjoying college and taking classes because they sounded interesting, not because it was a requirement for my major.

During my undergraduate career I spent a year abroad in Florence, Italy and Oxford, England where I was fortunate enough to study art and complete an internship at the Museum of Modern Art, Oxford, England. I received a BFA in Fine Art and have been creating art ever since.

When I returned to Seattle to finish my undergraduate degree I joined the Seattle based band Sky Cries Mary in which I am still involved. The band has put out 10 albums and toured internationally. We released albums under World Domination Records, Capitol Records, Warner Brothers Records and now our own independent label, Hoodooh Music. I also produced two solo albums under the name Hana. In 1993 I married my bandmate and fellow lead singer, Roderick Wolgamott, who subsequently took my name (Romero) in marriage.

In September of 2001 I moved with my husband Roderick to New York City to more fully pursue art and design. I attended graduate school at New York University and received my MA in Painting. I also received an associate degree in Interior Architecture from Parsons School of Design. Interior design was a career that had been naturally developing over the past decade. One of those jobs you "fall into" and fall in love with.

Roderick and I started Romero Studios Inc. in 2002. Our joint venture encompasses our many artistic projects including interior design, painting and treehouses. I have recently expanded into a new company, Anisa Romero Art and Design Ltd., which focuses exclusively on my own art and interior design.

In 2005 I was blessed with my daughter Petra Della Wolgamott Romero. She came 13 years into my marriage with Roderick. We all currently reside in New York City's East Village. We are artists, musicians and designers— and we wouldn't have it any other way.

When I was a teenager, I read Isadora Duncan's autobiography. I was stunned by her complete spiritual and artistic liberation. She seemed to possess a freedom from conformity, which inspired me. I marveled, and still do, that one can live their life with no regard for what is expected. She seemed to truly tap into the divine in all her artistic endeavors.

One of my more recent heroes is Sharon Gannon, a Yogi, poet and founder of the Jivamukti Yoga School. I first met Sharon when I was in my early years of college and she is now a dear friend and a teacher. In retrospect, she shares some similarities with Isadora Duncan: a complete artist and non-conformist. She started as a dancer and performance artist, and then merged into the realm of yoga's teachings and philosophy. Sharon studied the discipline for years, traveling to India and meeting an array of spiritual gurus and teachers. Over the years she has honed in on her own interpretation of the mystical and practical art of yoga, touching people around the world.

Sharon inspired me to get in touch with the world around me. She introduced me to the implications of vegetarianism, not just for my health, but also for the benefit of the environment and well-being of animals. Sharon has been an inspiration to me in the later part of my "growing up." She demonstrated to me that life could be lived with compassion and artistry.

Anisa Romero
139 Fulton Street - Suite 501
New York, NY 10038
anisa@anisaromero.com
646-295-3637

Annette M. Sanchez

Annette M. Sanchez, Inventor of The Veggie-Peel and Founder of Hometiquette, Inc., has always been an entrepreneur of sorts with a very inventive mind; always looking at how things work and figuring out ways they can be improved upon by one method or another.

She first conceived the idea for The Veggie-Peel several years ago as she watched a sitcom character making a tremendous mess while using a common peeler on television. She immediately thought, "There must be a better way!" and began working on developing a product that would eliminate the mess common peelers made.

After two years of research and design development, Annette became aware of a nationwide product search launched by QVC and *The Oprah Winfrey Show* entitled The Next Big Idea. She immediately submitted a request to present her product. In no time, she found herself on an airplane to Chicago where she demonstrated The Veggie-Peel to the QVC and *Oprah Winfrey* staffs for the first time. Out of over 7,000 products, The Veggie-Peel was one of only eight which were carefully selected to be presented on *The Oprah Winfrey Show* on May 3, 2007. The appearance on *The Oprah Winfrey Show* was an incredible experience and since the show aired, she has been contacted from people worldwide who are interested in buying or distributing this amazing new product.

In March of 2008, The Veggie-Peel completed the manufacturing and production phases and Sanchez began offering this product exclusively through her website at www.veggie-peel.com. In 2009, a DRTV distribution deal was signed with the number one pitchman in the world; however, before the commercial could be produced Annette was shocked to learn that he had passed away suddenly and unexpectedly in his sleep. Annette is currently seeking a national distributor to help sell this incredible product nationwide and is hopeful The Veggie-Peel will experience mass distribution in the near future!

———◆———

I was born in San Francisco, California in 1956 as the youngest of five children. My parents were born and raised on the Hawaiian island of Oahu, married in 1942 and eventually left the islands several years after the birth of my first brother Joseph and the Japanese attack on Pearl Harbor. They eventually made their way to San Francisco where my other siblings, Richard, David and Becky were born. Approximately three years after my birth, my family moved the 20 miles from San Francisco to Daly City, California which is where my parents settled in and my siblings and I ultimately grew up.

My brother David and I were very close and spent a lot of time together. My two oldest brothers were much farther apart in age than David, Becky and I so for the most part, the three of us spent most of our childhood together. As adults, all of us made a point to spend major holidays together, but since that was the only time we saw each other, for the most part we were strangers at best.

I graduated from Westmoor High School in 1974 and took a job in the credit card division of Bank of America as a fraud adjuster. I married a short time later and moved back to San Francisco in February 1975. That same year, I gave birth to my one and only child Maria Teresa, which was an incredible and life changing event. We began building a life together as a family but things did not work out and our marriage ended in December 1979. This began my journey as a single mom working at building my career through various well- known companies in the San Francisco Bay Area.

In 1982, we learned that my older brother David was diagnosed with a form of cancer called Hodgkin's, which was quite a blow to us all. He underwent a series of chemotherapies and ultimately went into remission. The doctors told him that if one stays in remission for 10 years with this type of cancer, they are considered cured, so we were all hopeful and prayed that he would stay healthy. We breathed a sigh of relief 10 years later, grateful that he would be around for a long time to come.

Sadly, in March of 1994 we learned that his cancer had returned and by November he was gone. This had a tremendous impact on the family and was the point when my siblings and I made a commitment to become closer and never miss a family celebration in years to come.

In 1995, my daughter Maria married her husband Leo which opened up a whole new chapter in my life— especially after she gave birth to my first grandchild, Amanda, in 1996. This was a wonderful time for me but also a very difficult one as I also had just fulfilled a long- time dream of becoming a realtor which required that I relocate to Roseville, California in order to ensure my success. After a lot of careful consideration, I made the decision to purchase a home in Roseville and thus began my full-time real estate career. I also became involved with the Roseville Chamber of Commerce and became an Ambassador for the Chamber participating in the grand openings of many new businesses throughout the area.

During the months to come I moved my parents to Roseville and my daughter and family visited me frequently. It didn't take long for them to realize that Roseville is a wonderful place to raise a family so they decided to take the plunge and purchase their first home there in 1997. Over the years, my two brothers, sister, nephew and many other family members relocated to the Roseville area where we all enjoy a much more affordable and fulfilling life.

In 1997, my brother Joseph became the second immediate family member to become stricken with cancer; this time Non-Hodgkin's lymphoma. After several months of chemotherapy his cancer was in remission but only for a short time. In 1998, his cancer came back in full throttle and he eventually had to undergo stem cell replacement therapy and a series of blood transfusions which required extended hospitalization. Fortunately, the treatments were effective and he has been in remission for nearly 10 years!

In 2001, I joined forces with a local property management firm to oversee the management of several apartment buildings in numerous outlying areas. Within two years, I was able to expand and develop my portfolio into a large multimillion dollar group of properties that included over 26 apartment communities throughout Northern California wherein I supervised a staff of over 40 employees. My dedicated service and hard work was a huge asset to the firm as it resulted in the establishment of a brand new regional office for the company.

Shortly thereafter in March of 2004, I decided it was time for me to enjoy some quiet time off to "reacquaint" myself with my family. So I did just that; however, within days I felt terribly fatigued and noticed a lump on the side of my neck. Knowing the medical history of my two other siblings, I immediately made an appointment with my doctor. A biopsy was quickly taken and within just a few days I received the terrible news: Non- Hodgkin's lymphoma, stage II indolent in nature or more commonly known as incurable cancer. My doctors quickly began scheduling a wide range of tests to determine the extent of the disease. Finally, the bone marrow test revealed the truth: the cancer had spread into my bone marrow escalating my diagnosis to stage IV.

My doctors immediately began formulating a treatment program that would span an eight month period of chemotherapy every three weeks beginning almost immediately. During this time, my 84-year-old father's own health conditions began to quickly deteriorate which required round-the-clock care.

By November 2004, the treatments concluded and my cancer was effectively in remission. Hallelujah! Life isn't over yet! It has now been four years since the chemotherapy sessions concluded and I praise the Lord my cancer is still in remission and inactive. Sadly, one month later my father Joseph Sr. passed away after a long battle with Alzheimer's disease.

I spent the next several years working as a regional property manager and realtor in the Roseville area until a life-changing moment of another kind occurred. By 2007, my real estate career in property management had blossomed and eventually afforded me the opportunity to focus on my inventing capabilities. This led to the creation of the innovative Veggie-Peel and the establishment of my company, Hometiquette, Inc.

On April 15, 2010, my mother, Ellen M. Sanchez, passed away at the age of 85 after several years of declining health. Although we were all terribly saddened by her passing, we were equally pleased to know that she and my father are together again.

I have had quite a few ups and down in my life but the most important thing is my family: my daughter Maria, my three grandchildren Amanda, Angelo and Alec, my wonderful son-in-law Leo, my two brothers Joseph and Richard, my sister Rebecca and my cat Smokey.

Growing up my heroes were people like Thomas Edison (inventor of the light bulb), Johannes Gutenberg (inventor of the printing press) and Alexander Graham Bell (inventor of the telephone) just to name a few. People with inventive minds fascinate me because I admired them for their wisdom and sharp minds. I myself have always looked at things with a different eye than most and love finding ways to improve upon things, be it gadgets or streamlining processes. It is more than just an interest in knowing how things work but rather a need to stimulate my own thought process and figure out ways to make things better. I find it quite interesting that my elementary school was name after Thomas Edison and I remember doing a book report on him when I was in first grade. In retrospect that was a "light bulb" moment for me!

The best words of wisdom come from those who have experience in this fascinating journey called Life. You must keep an open mind and listen to the voices of those who have already walked down whatever path you are preparing to take. Then listen to the voices in your heart so you can find the passion you will need to accomplish what you want in life. And finally, listen to the voices in your mind so you can use your intelligence to make sound decisions and achieve those goals. Then forge ahead with confidence and you will be successful!

photo by Harold Bailey, Jr.

Bernicestine McLeod Bailey

Bernicestine McLeod Bailey is currently the active Vice President of Aisha & Co LLC, a family business that specializes in the stationery, gift and toy industries. Bernicestine also founded McLeod Associates, Inc., an information technology consulting firm that currently specializes in performance management and business intelligence software applications. It is a company that has always dealt with data; recognizing the value of information and conveying that importance to clients.

She is a graduate of Brown University, and remains an active alumnus. She was elected to the Brown Corporation (the Board of Trustees) in 2001 and is currently a Trustee Emerita. She has been involved at Brown most recently as a Vice Chair of the Campaign for Academic Enrichment, specifically the Alumni of Color Initiative, as well as the past Chair of the President's Advisory Council on Diversity and Chair of the Archives Committee of the Pembroke Associates Council. Additionally, she has served as Class Treasurer and co- founded the Investment in Diversity Fund and the Third World Network. She is also involved in the Parents Council, several Reunion Gift Committees, Friends of the Library and the Third World Alumni Activities Committee as well as participating in numerous on- campus forums and seminars. She was an initial recipient of the Brown Alumni Service Award and received the Brown Bear Award for sustained alumni service in 2007, which was one of her most thrilling moments and a truly cherished honor.

In addition to her work at Brown, Bernicestine has served as President of the Fairfield/Westchester Chapter of the Independent Computer Consultants Association and recently completed two terms as a Trustee of the Westport Connecticut Public Library. She is the Director of the Fairfield County Community Foundation and currently serves as Secretary of TEAM Westport, whose mission is to achieve, extend and celebrate diversity in the town of Westport, Connecticut. Additionally, she recently completed terms as a Director on the boards of Dress for Success Mid-Fairfield County and REACH Prep, a scholastic program for low-income African American and Latino children from Fairfield (CT) and Westchester (NY) counties.

————◆————

My parents, Robert Leroy McLeod, Sr. and Wilhelmina Pinckney McLeod, moved from their birthplace in Sumter, South Carolina to Washington, DC, where I was born. I am the eldest of four children (three girls and a boy) and a member of the much discussed "Baby Boomer" generation. Growing up not too far from the United States Capitol and all of the institutions of our federal government in a mixed working-class/middle-class African-American neighborhood in Northwest Washington was, for the most part, rewarding. My parents both worked for the government: my mother for the Census Bureau and the Department of Agriculture, and my father for the US Postal Service which at that time was still an agency—not yet the quasi- private entity it is today.

At the time I was pretty much oblivious to the full impact of the federal government upon our lives. I was more concerned with the joys and the day-to-day challenges of being a child: school, dancing and piano lessons, church, friends and family. Still, I was able to partake of unique experiences such as riding the train under Capitol Hill that carried members of Congress (primarily men) back and forth between the Capitol and their offices—a treat not enjoyed by many. Now, due to security concerns, no one has public access like we had then. So I grew up being able to visit the museums, the parks, the granite monuments and to experience our government at work from my little window on the world. Walking to the main DC Public Library (now repurposed as the DC Historical Society) was one of my frequent pleasures.

As I look back now, the District of Columbia was an exciting and educational place in which to grow up. Although I moved away from Washington to attend college at Brown University and have not lived there since graduating, I try to get back there at least five times a year to visit. I changed my major from Mathematics to Economics at Brown, met my husband Harold Bailey, Jr., and worked summers at the Pentagon. Upon graduation, I went to work as a systems engineer at my first real place of employment—IBM's Wall Street office in New York City (and later in their manufacturing and distribution office in Boston). I held that position for 12 years. In New York, our clients were the brokerage houses and the New York Stock Exchange; in Boston they were manufacturers and distributors. In both places, I was one of the very few African-American women in a predominately white and male world. By working at a major corporation (IBM) I caught the wave of Civil Rights and Feminism at a time when the workforce was not very diverse. The contrast between this life (beginning at Brown University) and my life growing up was extreme. I went from the shelter of a totally African-American existence to the reality of an almost totally white world. Surprisingly, being in this environment at the apex of so many changes and opportunities for social activism seemed natural to me.

My two children (Aisha and Harold III) were born during my 12 years at IBM. I decided to leave IBM shortly after Harold was born and founded McLeod Associates, Inc., an information technology consulting firm. Throughout my professional career, travel has been a mainstay, and our family has been fortunate to experience many different cultures. We have lived in New England (Massachusetts and Connecticut) and in Texas. We also have extended family in many areas of the country: the Midwest, the South, and the Mid-Atlantic. We have visited various states and countries and have an appreciation for many different kinds of people and ways of life.

Professionally, I have always wanted to do community service and give back in some way. From early on, I have been an ongoing active volunteer for civic and community organizations in both leadership and participant roles. All of these "extra-curricular" pursuits reflect my lifelong interests in education, history and access and achievement for everyone. My early years have led me to this point with grace. I hope I have made my parents proud and that my children will continue to improve upon the legacy of service to others.

At this time I find myself aging gracefully, so for me the contemplation of my heroes growing up was quite an intriguing question upon which to reflect. In my relatively long life, I have encountered many who *might* be designated as "my heroes." I must state my true "she"roes/heroes who stand out above all the rest are many unsung women of African-American descent such as my mother, my teachers, my aunts and the women of my church who were my role models as I grew up.

My mother, Wilhelmina Pinckney McLeod, was a working mother (as were so many African-American women) who raised four children with my father and in later life has survived three bouts with breast cancer. She planted the seed in me that blossomed into my love for math and logic. Even today my chosen profession of information technology and my innate love of puzzles (which constantly accompany me on the road or when I'm in my favorite easy chair) bespeak the growth of that seed. She and my father both instilled within me the expectation that college and lifelong learning would be my destinations. She inspired us all to recognize and appreciate our uniqueness and to achieve all that we could and more.

Many of my teachers, including Ms. Drayton, Mrs. Holley, Miss Harvey (my high school Latin teacher and college counselor who guided me to look at the Ivy League for college) were stalwart posts along the road and all became integral parts of who I am.

In many ways, I feel I have been near the forefront of many trends—somewhat of a pioneer. The role models I mentioned above were those who gave me the values, beliefs and the character to realize that I could be strong, persistent, enduring and able to maintain my integrity no matter what the odds...while still being true to myself and to those important to me. So although very few of my "she"roes/heroes had college educations, their faith and perseverance, caring and resolve have sustained me and have helped me accomplish much during my time.

I was a child of the 1950s and early 1960s—growing up during the Civil Rights Movement, before the Feminist Movement. So although I was too young to be an active participant in the Civil Rights Movement, I received its benefits by being the first in my family and among the first African-American women in any numbers to receive an Ivy League education and degree. In addition, I was among the first African-American women to be hired by a major corporation in a position requiring technical skills (not just administrative skills) as Feminism was coming into vogue. Later, I would catch the entrepreneurial bug before the wave, and as I raised a family, used this vehicle to forge onward. I can only hint at how personally challenging these experiences were for me as I went through them. I knew, however, that failure was not an alternative and I am grateful that my "she"roes were ever-present and by my side in some respects through all.

The times have changed considerably. Growing up in the 1950s and 1960s was quite different from growing up now. Exposure to the media was different, as were those selected to be public icons. Access to the "outside world" was much more limited; communications and technology were much less extensive. During that time, families and local people—people with whom we came into direct contact every day—were extremely influential upon our thinking, our reactions and our world view. This is not to say that they aren't important in today's world; however, the chance for external, global factors to influence everyone today is much, much greater. Leaders, professionals and role models were white males, while women's roles were very defined and restricted. Consequently, heroes for women were few and the definition of heroes was different. In later life, I added Sojourner Truth and unsung women who struggled, lived and built to make it conceivable and possible for me to lay the foundation for my own children. Now we are able to include for younger women many visible examples in all walks of life who may be "she"roes; however, due to widespread media and the star quality that currently pervades, the "she"roes and heroes with whom we are presented are not always the most desirable and should be differentiated from true and appropriate role models.

The words of wisdom that I would impart to young girls today who are searching for their voices are: Go for it! It's a new day, behold! Roar!

We have made progress as women since the Feminist Movement began. There are many, many opportunities for women in all walks of life and women are more "free" in a sense to decide what they want to do. All is not totally equal *yet* when we compare the status of men to that of women in the workforce, but keep striving. Know thyself; define your passion.

Although life can be tough, do not give in or up for what is right for you and your family. Be persistent. As Malcolm Gladwell states in *Outliers, the Story of Success*, "The idea that excellence at performing a complex task requires a critical minimum level of practice surfaces again and again in studies of expertise. In fact researchers have settled on what they believe is the magic number for true expertise: ten thousand hours…Ten thousand hours is the magic number of greatness." So keep at it however you define "it."

Think of your community and your world as being your extended family and treat everyone as such. Seek out others of like mind and bond with them. Align yourself with the universe and all it has to offer. In all respects and circumstances, make your contribution to the greater good. Giving is receiving. Love and charity prevail always.

When you encounter roadblocks along your route, seek out alternate routes to your goal or wait temporarily until the road is clear again. Opportunity presents itself in many faces. Maintain your values always. Respect others and their accomplishments as you go along your way.

As a mother, I selfishly believe that giving the above advice to my children has played some part in the successes they have realized—especially not giving up when obstacles arose that might have prevented them from achieving their dreams. Their dreams were allowed to be bigger than mine, reflecting today's opportunities. I am proud that my daughter, Aisha, has realized two of her big dreams at quite an early age—physician and entrepreneur—while being a good person with strong values and lots of love to give. Now, I am not at all ashamed (actually quite elated) to say that I work for her and I am applying all of my life lessons to further *her* vision for the world since she and her children are the future. My son, younger than Aisha, is well on his way, too. For this I am extremely thankful.

CAROLE HOCHMAN

CAROLE HOCHMAN IS PERHAPS THE single most influential woman in the intimate apparel and sleepwear business in the United States today. She is the President and Creative Director of Carole Hochman Design Group.

A designer and industry pioneer, Carole Hochman has been designing intimate apparel for more than 30 years. What began as a young girl's dream to become a New York City fashion designer has today evolved into a global powerhouse company. The Carole Hochman Design Group manufactures not only the unsurpassed Carole Hochman brand of sleepwear, loungewear and daywear, but also owns OnGossamer and the licenses to several exceptional lingerie and sleepwear collections including Oscar de la Renta, Ralph Lauren, Jockey and Betsey Johnson.

Carole Hochman has always had an innate ability to identify opportunities, identify trends and translate designers' visions into successful intimate collections. She began her career in lingerie by accident. While attending Drexel University, a trade college in Philadelphia where she studied fashion design, she landed a job at Bergdorf Goodman in a department she'd given very little thought to before—lingerie. Carole worked hard, learned the business and was soon hired by a lingerie company and had the opportunity to design sleepwear for Bonwit Teller. Without knowing a thing about garment construction or the fabrics required to produce them, Carole nailed the collection on the first try, launching her career into the dreamy world of intimate apparel.

The following year, Carole Hochman began working for a small New York-based intimate apparel design firm. It was here she truly learned how to design collections that would satisfy both women's fantasies as well as their lifestyle needs—pioneering new directions for intimate apparel. In 1985, as a testament to Carole's vision and talent, the company was re-named Carole Hochman Designs.

During this time, Christian Dior was Carole Hochman Design's biggest licensee, and the industry standard in luxury lingerie. It was sold in virtually every major department and specialty store, and found in every elegant woman's wardrobe across America. Carole went several times a year to Paris mastering the art of flawless construction and experimenting with different textiles and fabrics.

Then, in the late 1980s, the economic downturn dictated a shift in the consumer mindset away from pure luxe and towards comfort. Carole instantly saw an opportunity to design sleepwear that revolved around comfortable-chic. She set her sights on Turkey, which was experiencing a cotton boom. Carole returned within weeks with a 100 percent cotton sleepwear collection that Macy's bought virtually sight unseen. Thus began the launch of the Carole Hochman brand of sleepwear that is today synonymous with luxury, comfort and style and sold in better department and specialty stores across the United States.

By the mid-'90s, Carole Hochman was renowned for her cotton knitwear and was approached by global fashion houses (including Espirit and Ralph Lauren) to design their sleepwear collections. She was one of the first designers to embrace the concept of QVC, recognizing the power of the home shopper—a customer who has proved loyal to her from the start. Today, The Carole Hochman Design

Group boasts a portfolio of brands, each with its own distinctive positioning and style, that together comprise an impressive segment of the better sleepwear and intimate apparel business.

The Carole Hochman Design Group is headquartered in New York City and run by Carole Hochman who is both President and Creative Director. Carole lives in Manhattan and has two children and four grandchildren.

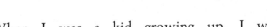

When I was a kid growing up, I was always crafty. I loved art…especially paper dolls. Those were my inspirations. As I got older and knew I was on my way to apply for college, I wasn't quite sure which direction to go. I thought perhaps Pharmacology, but luckily I chose design. I met a woman who was working in textiles for DuPont and since she attended Drexel University, that's where I decided to go. There I studied fashion and loved working with colors and textiles.

Some of my heroes growing up were many of the glamorous movie stars including Doris Day and Rock Hudson. Most impressive and inspirational was the legendary Jackie Kennedy.

My advice for the young women looking for their voices is: If you are lucky to connect to something you love, you can make it your career.

photo by M photo by Sara Allard

CHRISSY SPARROW

SOMETIMES A BAD HAIR DAY can inspire true creativity. Chrissy Sparrow, Creator of the Styl Styk Hair Part-ner, developed this innovative hair tool out of the need to combat grown out roots between coloring appointments.

After calling her local hair salon in Chagrin Falls, Ohio for an appointment, Chrissy discovered her stylist was completely booked and could not touch-up her roots. Luckily, Chrissy's stylist clued her in on a hairdressing secret often used by celebrity hairdressers: a zigzagged part, which hides dark roots and extends the look of hair color.

Chrissy loved the tip, but trying to achieve a professional result on her own at home proved to be a challenge. "I've spent many mornings in front of the mirror trying to part my hair like my stylist, but I could never quite get it right and always ended up being frustrated." Chrissy also tried other hair parting products, with little or no success which added to her disappointment.

Then one morning, when her usual rat tail comb could not be found, she grabbed an old hair pin from the bathroom drawer to part her hair. "I could not believe my eyes. My chin hit the floor; by mistake I had stumbled on a way that I could part my hair like a professional."

Chrissy's first prototype was her hair pin taped to one of her son's school pencils. She carried it with her always. Her husband, unbeknownst to her, hired an engineer to have a real prototype made (which he wrapped in her stocking and gave to her at Christmas).

She proudly began using her invention and learned that other customers at the salon were also struggling with trying to part their hair and in fact, would stop in for lessons. With the knowledge that others were having the same problem…the idea to create a new hairstyling tool to help women was born. Check out her invention at www.stylstyk.com.

Two of my biggest heroes growing up were my grandparents. They were Armenian and survivors of the Armenian Genocide. The most violent atrocities committed against the Armenians were between 1915 and 1921. Armenians were murdered, terrorized, placed under arrest and forced to leave their homeland. My grandparents and their families were farmers who owned vineyards to grow grapes for wine. They were forced to leave everything behind and go into hiding very similar to the experience of Anne Frank, a story many of us are familiar with.

I grew up with them telling me stories of how they had to wear corsets that they made themselves to hide their money and coins inside. The rubbing of the corsets caused chaffing and sores. My "Auntie" Rose was the oldest girl and had gone to finishing school in France. She spoke French and would go out to buy food and try to find someone to help them escape from the building that the rest of her family was hiding in. Eventually, a guard at the Turkish Embassy helped them escape. They paid him to take them on a wagon covered with hay to the shipyards so they could get on a boat that was headed for Greece. One by one, they immigrated to the United States.

My grandparents were never bitter about what they had witnessed and were always grateful to have escaped with their lives. The most important thing they taught me was to never lose faith in God—no matter how unbearable your situation may seem.

Another heroic influence was my mother. If you asked her what the first 13 years of her marriage to my father were like, she would describe it as "perfect" almost like "Doris Day." She and my father, along with their parents, started a retail business in a nice suburb outside of Cleveland, Ohio.

Everyone in the family worked together and made a good living. As my parents' family grew (I'm one of five children) my mother stayed at home with us, but continued to work from home by managing a huge Rolodex of their customers for billing and direct mail.

After the birth of my youngest brother my father left our home, and for various reasons could no longer be a husband to my mother or a father to his children. This was a very upsetting and unsettling time in all of our lives. I was 15 and totally shocked that my parents were getting a divorce. There was never any fighting or indication that anything was wrong with their relationship. They had been in counseling for several years, but the relationship ended in divorce.

My mother and father still worked together, which made things difficult. Eventually, my mother bought my father out of the business and took over the operations herself. She was a wonderful example of a woman that kept her family together and did whatever she could do to keep us in our house and in the community that we grew up in.

As I got older, I asked my mother how she managed to "keep it together" raising five kids and running a business on her own. Being a mother myself, with only one child, as well as having a loving and supportive husband, I was amazed that she was able to hold it all together. She told me that she could remember going into our backyard behind the bushes, falling to her knees crying, just wanting to die. She thought about her history and where her parents had come from…what they had endured armed only with their faith in God. She realized then that she was a survivor too and could stand up and face any fear that came her way. It would be her faith that would see her through.

I struggled as our family life changed. After the divorce, instead of facing the changes that were happening, I chose to just ignore the situation. I didn't want to talk to my parents, a counselor or anyone else for that matter. Instead, I avoided my personal loss and dealt with all of the hurt and pain by suppressing my feelings. I still can remember making a conscious decision to just "turn off my feelings" and pretend that the divorce never happened and then everything would be okay. Boy was I wrong!

My mom was not big on "dating" but did go out occasionally. One night, a family friend asked my mom to go out with her to dinner. She reluctantly went and on that night, ran into a man that her friend had gone to school with. And as fate would have it, this man (who was also divorced with five kids!) would one day become her husband, my stepfather, and another hero in my life.

During these years, in my middle to late teens, I was exposed to drugs and alcohol at school and at parties. I wasn't that into drugs, even though I had a lot of friends at school who were smoking pot, taking pills and trying cocaine. Luckily, I had a fear that I would become "hooked" on drugs and end up being a drug addict. So, I basically stayed away from the drugs and began experimenting with alcohol.

Well, I quickly found that I loved to drink! When I drank, I could "escape" from the world and I was taken to a place where I just felt good. There was no "pain" and the best part was that it made pretending the divorce didn't happen a lot easier.

I went off to college (because I did not know what else to do) and I loved the freedom of being away from home. My high school grades were not very impressive, but I thought that I would be able to handle the workload if I really applied myself. At first things were fine, but when drinking and looking for "Mr. Right" became the reason that I was there, my grades became less important and suffered.

I spent three years on and off academic probation each and every semester. I really don't know how I managed to stay in school that long. I had started to experience blackouts (loosing track of hours or time) and began to realize that when I picked up any kind of alcoholic drink, I had no control over how much I drank, or what I did when I was under the influence of alcohol.

I would have never dreamed in a million years that all of the pain that I would experience in my teens and early twenties was necessary to get to where I am today!

Years ago, if you would have told me that I was going to become estranged from my father, become an alcoholic, drop out of college, get sober, go back to school, graduate with honors, become a certified welder, work for a wonderful internationally known company, be introduced to my future husband by my stepfather, get married, have a wonderful son, stumble on and invent a helpful hairstyling tool, develop it with the help of my stepfather, get on QVC, HSN, appear on The Big Idea with Donny Deutsch and then find a greater purpose for my invention when a national breast cancer organization reached out to me, I would have said, "Are you totally nuts?!" but that's my story and it all happened.

Looking back, I can see that this was the way God intended my life and my "heroes" lives to be and I am grateful that He helped us all survive and find our way.

I would tell young girls today to trust in a "Power" that is outside of yourself. For me, that "Power" happens to be my faith in God. But you can use the wonder of Nature, the Universe or any other Spiritual idea that you can believe in but not fully understand the concept behind or reason for. For example; the sun sets and rises each day. How does that miracle happen? Even without knowing why, I can count on the sun rising and setting each day.

Take pride in your work. Do the best job you are capable of doing. Whether it's doing your homework or getting cleaned up to get going for your day, do the best that you can do. It will make you feel good about yourself.

Be open to new ideas. Trust your instincts, but don't hold yourself back by believing that you know all of the right answers and ideas. Love yourself enough to know that you have limits!

And lastly, if you think that you may have a problem with drugs or alcohol, you probably do. Don't be afraid or ashamed to trust in others and ask for help.

photo by Mike Hemberger

DAWN JUNEAU

DAWN JUNEAU IS THE CO-OWNER of Pump Wear Inc. (www.pumpwearinc.com) where children and adults with type I diabetes can find fun and creative ways to wear their insulin pumps. Pump Wear gives back to many diabetes organizations, and the website includes a forum for families to communicate and offer support to those with a connection to diabetes. Dawn and her business partner, Julie Defruscio, have expanded the company into a second venture, Girly Girl Studios, where customers can design their own handbags at www.girlygirlstudio.com.

———◆———

I grew up in Cohoes, New York and attended Catholic Central High School in Troy, New York. After graduating HVCC I went to work for

GE in Schenectady, NY where I have worked for 30 years. I still remember my interview with the recruiter. We talked about guys and diamonds. It taught me at an early age that interviews are not always what you expect them to be. Being able to adapt is as important in a job interview as it is in owning your own business. One reason I went to work for GE was the benefit of obtaining my degree and having the company pay for it. I achieved that goal in 2007 and got my Marketing/Management degree. This fulfilled a promise I made to my mother.

At 38 years old I found myself facing what many women have now faced…breast cancer. I was diagnosed with stage II and underwent a lumpectomy and then eight aggressive chemotherapy and 31 radiation treatments. When things get difficult for me I remember the conversation I had with my surgeon when I asked him if I was going to die. Dr. Hena looked at me and said, "Yes, but not from this." It was my moment of reckoning with this disease and allowed me to understand that this was merely a minor "glitch" in my life. I can now look back 12 years later and say that the year I was diagnosed was in fact one of the best years of my life. The support from family and good friends is important. Losing my parents was hard, surviving cancer was easy.

I met Al Juneau, my future husband, at Julie's son Adam's birthday party. I am now the proud mother to two wonderful stepchildren: Jennifer and Justine. My other "babies" are Lucky, a Norwegian elkhound who found my breast cancer (Lucky has since passed in 2008), Lucy, a mix of golden/German shepherd and a new baby Kara Belli who is a beautiful golden retriever born in February 2009.

Growing up my favorite hero was Jacqueline Kennedy. I was in awe of her life and the grace she showed under very difficult times. My love of reading made it easy to find out everything I could about this amazing lady.

Growing up my father was my hero. He taught me that if you want something bad enough, you will find a way to make it happen. Persistence and patience can get you far in life, and you don't have to take no for an answer. I remember my parents giving me a magical childhood of Christmases where we would go to bed at night and "Santa Claus" would not only decorate the house, but also bring the Christmas tree and gifts.

Looking back, I don't know how they were able to accomplish this in one night. Their love and devotion to the spirit of the holiday are memories that bring a smile to my face. The other legacy my parents left us is the important bond of family.

If there is any advice I could give young woman today, it would be to listen to your gut feelings. They will serve you well in guiding you through tough decisions. Always be true to this feeling; it will not let you down. Never be afraid to ask questions or ask for help. When someone says no to you, it is an opportunity to change their mind!

Another key thing for me is trust your business partner. If you cannot trust them, why be in business together? Julie and I were best friends before we started our business and have always maintained our friendship; it is the most important thing for us. Luckily for us, we bring out the best in each other. We recognize our strengths and weaknesses and trust our gut feelings.

DIANE LANG

MY HEROES GROWING UP: IN all honesty, I didn't have any. I think this is part of the hard part of growing up for me. I never had anyone to look up to. A lot of my friends had parents to look up to, but that wasn't my case. I didn't have many people in my life as the youngest of five with a huge age gap. My parents didn't socialize much with family and friends. I felt very isolated and alone as a child. I wish I had heroes, but I didn't.

Words of encouragement for young girls: Make sure to be yourself and not spend your life looking for acceptance and approval from others. I, unfortunately, made this choice. I picked a career choice that I hoped would be bring me fame so everyone would notice that I was special and would like me. It wasn't a career that brought me any happiness, and because it wasn't the right career for me, I never received the fame that I was looking for. If anything, it brought me down and made me feel worse about myself. I wasn't being my true self.

No matter what age you are, be you! Don't try to find acceptance or approval from others. Love yourself. The biggest fear we have is being unloved and unworthy. If we can learn in our younger years that we are always enough and loved, we could take away years of pain and wrong choices.

My mentor was my brother. He was a counselor and led me into the field. My brother was my biggest fan and always told me that I would be a good writer and to pursue it. I didn't for the first part of my life (teens and 20s) because I was too busy looking for acceptance from others. When I finally let go of that, my writing started to blossom, and I have written two books of my own and been part of a third book co-written with others. My brother was my biggest mentor and help.

Diane Lang — Therapist, Educator, and Life Coach

Therapist, Educator and Life Coach Diane Lang has dedicated her career to helping people turn their lives around and is now on a mission to help them develop a sustainable positive attitude that can actually turn one into an optimist, literally. A therapist and educator/coach of Positive Psychology, she has seen that it can provide a strong foundation for finding great happiness and is gratified that it is becoming a mainstream method of treatment.

A parent herself, Lang has taught Positive Parenting to parents and written extensively on the benefits of using it with even the youngest children. She has also spoken or conducted seminars on postpartum depression, striving for balance versus having it all, and practical tips on interviewing, networking, and dressing for success. She is the author of *Baby Steps: The Path from Motherhood to Career.*

Diane is a Therapist and Life coach in New Jersey. Her clinical experience includes treating patients with different forms of mental illness, physical and emotional abuse, and relationship issues. Lang is also an Adjunct in Psychology at Montclair State University. Her college work includes mentoring students for individual career counseling and personal issue advisement.

As an expert in her fields of therapy, Lang has been featured in the *Daily Record, Family Circle, Family Magazine, Working Mother Magazine, and Cookie Magazine*, seen on NJ 12 TV, *Good Day CT*, CBS TV, *Style CT*, the Veira network, and the national television program *Fox & Friends*. She has also participated in a reality based Internet show, *OurPrisoner*, hosted Generation X-tinet, and appeared in various educational videos, including Columbia books.

Lang has an M.A. in Counseling and a B.A. in Liberal Arts from the New York Institute of Technology. Diane has her Positive Psychology coaching certificate from Wholebeing Institute. Diane's latest book is *Creating Balance & Finding Happiness*.

Please visit her website for more information: www.dlcounseling.com

Or email: DLCounseling2014@gmail.com

DR. KATHLEEN HANDS

I WANTED TO BE A doctor at the age of four. Everything I did was toward that goal. My science projects were all medically related, dealing with pacemakers or comparing dog blood to human blood through the use of ticks. I got the highest award for science on graduation from high school in a small little town called Rockaway, New Jersey. I wasn't the smartest, but I was dedicated— true and unwavering—toward my future goal. I got the science scholarship to go to Marquette University in Milwaukee, Wisconsin. I was awarded early acceptance into medical school after my second year. All I had to do was complete one more year, but my mother took ill, and I moved back to New Jersey to care for her.

Opportunity gone, I applied to the CMDNJ (College of Medicine and Dentistry New Jersey) Physician Assistant Program. I was accepted and finished in three years, getting a BS and PA degree. Of course, in 1979, New Jersey was the only state where PAs were not legislated to practice medicine, and I was forced to move to Pennsylvania. There I set out to practice with the hopes of again applying to medical school.

In 1985, I applied and was accepted to the Medical College of Pennsylvania. I was in my first semester when life just happened. I left medical school again to take care of my mother, and met my husband Michael and married in 1986. I continued working as a physician assistant. He wanted children, and I wanted medical school. So I put my agenda on the back burner with the agreement that when the last child was on the school bus, I could go back to medical school. Unfortunately, his infertility issues prevented us from getting pregnant for three years. I could have finished medical school!

My children were born in 1989, 1990, and 1992, and when the youngest turn five years old (1997), I was able to go back to medical school, only this time I was told I was too old and should pick a new career. I was devastated but determined.

In 1997 at the age of 40, I went to a Caribbean medical school where age did not matter. It was a barbaric setup. We lived in old abandoned army barracks with tin roofs, goats, and chickens roaming the grounds with tree frogs croaking all night long. I was naïve and did not understand that coming back to the USA as a foreign grad would be a significant undertaking.

I was met with much discrimination, despite my excellent scores and testing in the top one percentile in both clinical and academia. I was deemed a Caribbean grad not worthy to attend medical clinics only worthy of United States medical students. Every rotation was fraught with discrimination and having to prove myself. Yet in every rotation, I was granted in A, with comments stating: *goes above and beyond, excellent role model, recommend highly for residency.*

When the time came for match, the biggest day in medical school, I chose an institution close to home as I was commuting one and a half hours each way every day to get to my clinical rotations. Working eighteen-hour days to prove myself and hoping that a residency closer to home would allow me time to see my family. I was matched at the institution I wanted in Camden, New Jersey, and on the first day of residency, I was told the school I went to was no longer recognized, and I would not be allowed to do my residency in that institution.

Match day is the most important day, which makes your career, and I had nowhere to go. It was 2001, I was forty-five years old, had placed in the top one percentile in the nation on board exams, and I had no residency. Total bewilderment overcame me. It was even too late for scramble. Scramble was for those who didn't get spots, who were not good enough or wanted, and were able to fill in the few extra spots that might be available in the dregs of America. I immediately called Christiana Care Hospital, where I had done a number of my medical clerkships, and spoke to Dr. Ginger C., the residency director. She was a very well respected E.F. Hutton type. When she spoke, everyone listened, like she carried a big stick. Her initial comment to me was being upset that I had not put Christiana Care down as a possible site for residency because she had filled the twelve spots with lesser residents, and was very disappointed that I was not one.

I was more bewildered than one could imagine. They had given me such a hard time through two years of medical clerkships, and here they wanted me to stay, and I could not. I would now have to wait another year? Six hours later the phone rang... It was Dr. C. She was able to call the powers that be and obtained funds to hire a thirteenth resident. I had a home.

I worked very hard those three years, still dealing with much discrimination and having to prove myself. I worked very hard and became chief resident. My husband was being transferred to Texas, and the decision for the future was coming fast. I could have stayed in Delaware and had a wonderful practice with wonderful doctors. Moving to Texas would mean starting over. I decided to do an endocrine fellowship. I had interviewed with the program director, during my second year of residency and absolutely enjoyed the prospect of being an endocrinologist under her tutelage.

I matched at University of Texas Health Science Center San Antonio for an endocrine fellowship. During the first week, I was informed that a training license would not be issued to a foreign medical graduate. Once again, I had won a prestigious seat, and I was being prevented from being a doctor and obtaining a license. The program director was furious. The match was over. There were no fellows to fill my spot … she persecuted me. Once again I contacted Dr. C. to explain my plight, and she took it upon herself to expedite a Delaware license, as it is easier to obtain a state license if you were already licensed in another state. She went out on a limb for me. She didn't have to do that.

Well, it took fights and arguments and discussions and letters. The state board had never issued a temporary license for a Caribbean grad, and they weren't going to start now. Once again bewildered and embarrassed that no matter how good you are, or how smart you are, or how well liked you are, it didn't matter. Dr. C. contacted the state medical board and communicated to them they need to have physicians like myself practicing medicine, and that I could only make the state of Texas proud.

It took three months, but they granted me temporary license. Unfortunately, the program director was so upset that she never spoke to me again, and when she did it was with utter disdain. She gave me extra call, she gave me extra duty, she gave me extra work, and she did everything in her power to break me. To this day I cannot wear a pager. I equate it to a post-traumatic stress disorder. I never felt hate from anyone before.

When I completed by fellowship, I was requested by Dr. D. to stay on at the Texas Diabetes institute in his division of diabetes. We assumed that since a training license was issued, a permanent license would be feasible. Unfortunately, that was not the case, and yet again I was turned down for a license in the state of Texas to practice medicine.

Dr. D is not someone to take no for an answer and forced the university to pay legal fees for me to fight the medical board to obtain a Texas medical license. It is the second hardest state in which to obtain a medical license. The hoops one must jump through and the regulations placed upon you are incendiary. Despite having school transcripts sent from the Caribbean for medical clerkships, internship, residency, and fellowship, the state board required yet another set of transcripts, which were not going to be released from the school. Sheer frustration—so close yet so far. I felt humiliated and embarrassed that if the state board doesn't recognize me how would anyone ever take me seriously. Suddenly it didn't matter how smart I was, or how hard I worked, my future was in the hands of the bureaucracy.

I had kept in touch with a few people from my past. One person in particular was my first diabetic patient as a PA. She was older than I was and wiser. She had broad shoulders and she cared deeply for me. She credits me for saving her life; she was in a diabetic coma when I first encountered her. She was smart and funny and I loved making rounds in the hospital to see her. We became good friends. I often went to her house, her log cabin, and had a cup of tea in the woods, and truly relaxed. I missed those days. I missed Liz. I would call her and tell her the latest chapter and verse, and she always made me feel better. She always made me feel it was just one more hurdle--that I was going to be triumphant and she was always there to help me.

I recently came upon all the letters she wrote to the state congressmen and senators of Texas, pleading my case, imploring them to intervene to allow me to get this license as she knew firsthand what an amazing doctor I was. We got no reply and time was running out. The school was not cooperating; it was out of the lawyers' hands, and without my transcripts, I could go no further. We contemplated getting on a plane and going to Antigua, but the island was so corrupt and the school was locked down, so I knew we would never gain entrance.

They wanted money; a lot of money. Yes, we call that extortion in the states, but that's how things are done. I was plum out of money. But Liz was not going to hear of this. We talked and made jokes about how we could get this information. We laughed and said we should be Thelma and Louise, have converted names that no one listening to our phone conversations could know what we were doing. We swore to secrecy. We swore we would never tell anyone.

I told her she was crazy and we could not do that, but in my heart I so hoped she would do just that. She contacted the school and pretended she was a Texas medical board licensing official and told the school dean that if they sent the transcripts, their school would be recognized as the first Caribbean school to allow a Texas license be granted to a Caribbean graduate. Up to that point no Caribbean grad had ever been granted licensure in the state of Texas. This was a very attractive tool to discuss with the dean, which would help legitimize their school, something that was very difficult to do in the Caribbean.

One week later, Liz called me and told me what she had done. I told her she shouldn't have done that. In my heart, I was so grateful that she had taken the bull by the horns and had something so brazen, but I was scared to death I would get caught. Four days later, the Texas State Board granted me a medical license in the state of Texas. I cried for days. Thelma, as I refer to her now, was able to get her favorite doctor to the front of the class and be granted a license to practice medicine. I might still be holding my breath had she not done that.

So Dr. D 's efforts paid off. I was hired at the Texas Diabetes Institute as an endocrinologist, and I thought all my woes were behind me. Unfortunately, the program director continued to torment me and cause trouble for me and never accepted that I was hired on as an endocrinologist. If I didn't know better, I would assume she did everything in her power at the state level to prevent me from getting that license. She went so far as to tell other physicians and other departments that I was a junior fellow despite being faculty, and to be leery of treating my patients. Little did I know, one of my colleagues and her partner, was intervening behind the scenes in communicating with those other physicians to let them know that I was bright and honorable and the best endocrinologist he knew—that he trusted my judgment unconditionally. This did not stop her behavior, which I discussed with my superiors, who laughed it off and told me to ignore it. My patients were being affected, which was very upsetting to me.

I sought legal counsel to write a letter to her to cease and desist her slanderous remarks and spreading rumors of my incompetency. We wound up in mediation—again an extremely uncomfortable, embarrassing, and humiliating experience. I was very successful in my faculty post, having started the thyroid clinic, was lecturing, teaching, publishing, and I begged her to accept my accomplishments as her own. I told her she was my mentor and she should be proud of me and not tear me down for I am a reflection of her! But she continued to slander, and I had no recourse.

I went to my superiors. I went to their superiors. I went to the head of the university. I explained that the treatment rendered to my patients was inappropriate. I showed them all the data to back up my points and showed them all the guidelines supporting not doing what they were doing to my patients. But I was told to shut up or get out. That university—where the standard of care was forty years behind the times, and no one was interested in the current standard of care—rendered suboptimal and even harmful care.

Never focus on how stressed you are; instead be grateful for how blessed you are.

By the end of my fourth year as faculty, having bucked the system to improve patient care, I remained unsuccessful and tendered my resignation. I set out to solo practice where I was told I would fail, go broke, and come crawling back. My father always taught me to do the right thing no matter how unpopular or how painful. In my heart, I knew that as long as I was doing best care for patients I would be successful.

I opened my practice on September 7, 2010. By December 30, 2010, I was fully booked and have been since. My reputation precedes me. I have been invited to speak locally, nationally, and internationally. By January 2012, I was booked every week for a speaking engagement six months in advance. My office hours are on Monday, Tuesdays, and

Wednesdays, and I travel doing speaking engagements on Thursdays and Fridays.

In April 2015, I was asked to become the cover girl for San Antonio women's magazine. This is an honor bestowed upon six women in a given year that are recognized for contributions they make to society.

Although I am a doctor specializing in thyroid disorders only, I see a significant amount of overweight patients who think their primary problem is thyroid disease. Of course, eighty percent of these people do not have a thyroid condition and need help understanding how they became overweight. We spend a good deal of time discussing their physical health and what we can do to help them improve their health. Last year in my clinic, we lost 2517 pounds—a total of over 7000 pounds since we've been keeping track four years ago. This has gained me notoriety as a compassionate physician—a physician of conviction who is dedicated to my patients. I witness the "paying it forward" phenomenon, where these patients have inspired coworkers, spouses/partners, children, parents, and friends to lose weight and get healthier. Every patient expresses how they have been able to make a difference in someone else's life.

It has been a long journey, and maybe a necessary journey. I have always known this is where I belonged. Many times I have wanted to throw in the towel, but pure determination has kept me going. I'm fulfilled beyond any means I thought possible in my heart and in my soul. Being paid to do what I do is just a bonus. The real joy comes from the patients I help.

It only takes one person in your life to make or break you. How you respond to those individuals is your character. Never lower yourself to their level; always raise yourself up to be a better person in God's eyes. Surround yourself with positive people. Avoid those who do not cherish your every success. Remember: life is too short to spend it with people who stomp the happiness out of you. If God brings you to it, God will bring you through it.

One of the great lessons Liz taught me was in order to thrive in life, you need three bones: A wishbone, a backbone, and a funny bone.

Some of my favorite sayings include:

Good things don't come to those who wait; they come to those who work their asses off and never give up.

And remember, what doesn't kill you makes you stronger.... Except jersey girls—they will kill you!

I don't know how my story will end, but nowhere will it ever read... I gave up.

ELAINE GORDON

ELAINE GORDON IS THE FOUNDER of Elaine's American Maid and a perfect example of the American Dream. She started her business from nothing, and through sheer hard work and perseverance was able to lift herself and her family out of poverty, buy her dream house and reach out to help other struggling women at the same time.

Elaine also started Maid for Work which furthers her mission to help lower income women open their own housecleaning businesses to support themselves and fuel their dreams of becoming whatever they want to become. Elaine created Maid for Life, an organization which provides free housecleaning services for those struggling with cancer. Find more information on Elaine Gordon at www.elainegordon.org.

My name is Elaine Gordon and my rags-to-riches story shows that achieving the American dream takes a little dreaming, but mostly a lot of hard work and a call to action.

I am the founder of Elaine Gordon Consulting, a Board Certified Integrative Nutritional Specialist in private practice, and a graduate of the Institute For Integrative Nutrition in New York City.

Writing the recipes for the City Magazine in El Paso, Texas, on a monthly basis and also being a contributor for several of their featured stories, has been exciting to me because as a writer and an advocate for health and fitness, I am able to make real change in the community where I live and serve.

I am also the owner and operator of Intraceuticals Oxygen Infusion Spa, the only oxygen beauty treatment for the face, body, and hands in my city. I also do oxygen inhalation aromatherapy treatments to add health and vitality and relaxation for the body.

I began as an entrepreneur at the age of 19, launching Elaine's American Maid (elainegordon.org) in Florida and later in Washington State. I have been in business for myself and have launched thousands of other women in their own house cleaning businesses for more than 40 years.

More of my past work includes owning and operating Elaine Gordon's Production and Public Relations Firm, producing work including the short documentary film THE HEROES OF GROUND ZERO, which was nominated for an Emmy.

In order to change as many lives as possible for the better, I also started two foundations: Maid For Work, which launched low-income women into their own successful housecleaning business as independent entrepreneurs; and Maid For Life, which was started to provide free housecleaning services for women suffering from cancer.

While living in Washington State, I served on the Board of the Washington State Attorney General's Task Force for Domestic Violence and also sat on the board of the Traumatic Brain Injury Association. I now live and base my work out of El Paso, Texas, the world's largest border community and one of the fasted-growing in its commitment to healthy living.

I received my training as a Health Coach from the Institute for Integrative Nutrition's cutting-edge Health Coach Training Program.

During my training, I studied over 100 dietary theories, practical lifestyle management techniques, and innovative coaching methods with some of the world's top health and wellness experts. My teachers included Dr. Andrew Weil, Director of the Arizona Center for Integrative Medicine; Dr. Deepak Chopra, leader in the field of mind-body medicine; Dr. David Katz, Director of Yale University's Prevention Research Center; Dr. Walter Willett, Chair of Nutrition at Harvard University; Geneen Roth, bestselling author and expert on emotional eating; and many other leading researchers and nutrition authorities.

My education has equipped me with extensive knowledge in holistic nutrition, health coaching, and preventive health. Drawing on these skills and my knowledge of different dietary theories, I work with clients to help them make lifestyle changes that produce real and lasting results.

I grew up on welfare, started working at nine years old and became a single mom at age 19. When a health crisis left me without a way to provide for my baby, I started a business that would become Elaine's American Maid, which cleaned about 140 homes per week and provides work to about 80 mostly low-income women.

Through my entrepreneurship, I traded welfare for a million-dollar home in Redmond, Washington, where I lived as a single mother with my three children. My daughter Shavawn, 37, was a nanny for Madonna for nearly 10 years and is now a creative clothing stylist for Madonna and others in the film and music industries. My son Paul, 28, is an accomplished filmmaker and author. My youngest son Jonathan, 24, earned a bachelor's degree in Composition and Arranging at The Master's

College in Southern California. He recently arranged and recorded several albums and has composed music for Madonna's documentary, I Am Because We Are, and also composed and arranged music for Louis Vuitton and Dolce & Gabbana. Not only did I launch myself and my children out of poverty, but I also have taken on many other endeavors as well.

I grew up living in New York City on welfare. I had a mom who wasn't able to work because she was ill. I spent most of my young life taking care of her, and she died when I was 18 of heart disease. I feel like I grew up at age nine. I started ironing shirts for a nickel each. I was poor, but never felt poor in spirit. I looked around and saw the gold in the rocks, the opportunities. I knew the way to get to Park Avenue or the Plaza was through hard work.

I cleaned houses, babysat, ironed shirts, worked in an office at 14 years old—anything I could do to make money and teach myself the principles of being successful. My mother was the most encouraging person in the world. She said, "Elaine, you can do whatever you want to do. I believe in you." I think that's how I made it—through her words and her love.

I didn't really like New York after my mother died, so I went to Florida at age 19 and found myself pregnant with my daughter Shavawn. I said to myself, I am not going to be a second-generation welfare mom. I am not. So I started cleaning houses, but I was so young and naïve, I ended up with a collapsed lung and in the hospital (from breathing in fumes of a cleaning chemical). I had to support my 18-month-old baby and serve my customers, so I called all my friends who I knew were single moms, and asked them to clean my customers' homes.

Inside six months, I had 95 people working for me, servicing 156 houses a week. I was behind a desk interviewing people constantly. My job had become a business. I advertised in the paper. On the East Coast, everyone uses house cleaners. I got 50 calls a day. I had several answering services who didn't want to take care of me because my phones rang too much.

In the beginning, I didn't have a penny. I started my business on a shoestring. I threw an ad in the paper, put one foot in front of the other, and the business developed from there. That's why I enjoy working with low-income women, because you hardly need anything to start your own housecleaning business. You really can make something from nothing.

My mission is helping low income women across America to open their own housecleaning services to support themselves. I want to help all women who just want to survive. Then I want to launch them in their second businesses…what they really want to do, what they want to be when they grow up. They know how to make things work and how to survive with nothing. Give them a few tools and they are going to be the most phenomenal entrepreneurs you have ever seen.

What I'd really like to do is launch nationwide; not so much to license or franchise, but to go into cities and have seminars and teach women how to open their own housecleaning businesses or any other businesses that they feel drawn to. I would charge a comparable fee, but would want the women to find sponsorships to attend the seminar, maybe from government grants, churches or caring friends and family.

I have also started Maid for Life, a foundation that gives away free housecleaning to women with cancer, men who have just lost their wives to cancer, or parents whose children are dying of cancer. People are always wondering what they can do for someone who has cancer. Help them clean their house. A clean home signifies order in a chaotic life.

I have been donating housecleaning services to women with cancer and to men whose wives have died of cancer for several years now. I have been underwriting the cost myself. I would say that over the last several years, hundreds and hundreds of people have called me.

I also started Maid for Work which encourages low- income women to open their own house cleaning services, which allows them to provide for themselves and their families while at the same time returning home by the time their children get home from school. I believe that our children need us to be more readily available for their needs. One way to accomplish this, especially as a single mother, is by going into your own entrepreneurial business, which makes it easier for you to be more available when they get home from school.

My next project was branding myself. That's why I worked 15 hours a day to keep my doors open. I wanted to make some major steps besides going nationwide. I wanted to go on television and do talk shows around the country and brand myself as a cleaning expert...the next Domestic Diva, or as my friend nicknamed me, "The Queen of Clean." A cleaning show with many interesting guests would be a fun way to learn not only how to keep yourself and your home organized but also to get a jump start on exciting new entrepreneurial opportunities.

I also want to be a guest cleaner on shows like Martha, The View, et cetera. I developed a 30-minute workout that teaches you how to clean up the house before company comes or in between your maid service, and get an aerobic workout at the same time. I have worked with an exercise physiologist and a sports medicine doctor. I have put together a housecleaning and workout video that is currently awaiting distribution.

Housecleaning isn't so much about what gets out what spot on the rug. I want to talk to women frankly about their issues behind closed doors and how they relate to housecleaning. I find that the more women complain about housecleaning, the more they have other issues. Sometimes women would call me up screaming and yelling about just a little dust behind the toilet, and I would wonder, "Why are you losing it over this?" It's because the American woman today has way too much on her plate.

In order to be happy with your house cleaner, communication is key. If you're not able to communicate what you want, you're not going to get what you want. Where there are a lot of problems, it's usually because clients are not able to communicate with the house cleaner about what gets them excited, whether it's clean floors or the kitchen or the bathroom.

Financially, I have been extremely successful. I bought a house all by myself that's worth almost $1 million, in a Seattle area which is like the street of dreams. When I bought the house, my neighbors looked at me and said "What is a single mother doing in this neighborhood?" They did not get me at all.

I want to be able to use my dream house as a platform. When low-income women come in, I let them know, "This is America. This is my story. This is possible for you, too." I'm humbled to live here. But I don't sit back comfortably like I could not lose it. I have to continue to work hard.

My greatest successes are the Cinderella stories. Taking a woman who has no self-esteem, is completely downtrodden and distraught, and looking at her and telling her how amazingly beautiful and talented she is, and how I'm going to work to bring that out. The most amazing Cinderella stories happen. When women came into my office, their shoulders were drooped. Often they came out of domestic violence. In two months' time, these women bounce in and out of my office. All because I believed in them and gave them the tools to unlock the secrets inside themselves. That's been my greatest joy. That's why I got out of bed every morning.

My greatest challenge is the occasional screaming customer. Getting up every day and continuing on with the job I've done for 30 years. There are some days when customers have very naughty behavior. There's no reason for a woman to ever hyperventilate, to scream and swear and yell at anyone over housecleaning problems that are fixable. We need to be more understanding and more flexible and not be afraid to give someone the benefit of the doubt.

In the great words of Winston Churchill: "Never, never, never give up." Keep on keeping on. It will happen as long as you don't quit. You might take a breather, but no quitting. I believe in the saying, "If you have the idea or the inclination… just go do it." I freelance as a photojournalist and went to Ground Zero with my son Paul three weeks after 9/11, which helped to cultivate his career as a filmmaker. I made all the arrangements, not knowing how we were going to get access to Ground Zero. Meanwhile, Paul was finishing a film project with the

Redmond Police Department, and he told the Police Commander he was filming. The Commander said, "We're leaving for New York tomorrow. My best friend is the head of public relations for the city of New York Police Department. Your media passes will be ready." The press pass just fell out of the sky. The Library of Congress deemed the piece we filmed a historical document. It was nominated for an Emmy. When we returned from Ground Zero, we were all over the local Seattle television news. If you have the idea, the inclination or the fire inside of you to go do something, just go do it.

Now, after many years of battling with the state of Washington concerning low- income women becoming employees rather than sole proprietors, I decided to take on the state of Washington and challenge them. Their point was that because "individuals come from a low-income background...these individuals (low-income mainly single mothers) neither have the knowledge nor the capability" of ever running their own entrepreneurial businesses. After battling with the state for four years and spending tens of thousands of dollars opposing them and fighting for the rights of the low-income single mother as well as women and men as sole proprietors, I decided to close my doors after 25 years of faithful service to the people of the state of Washington and transfer my entire business over to all the house cleaners who have been a part of Elaine's American Maid.

I just recently lost my case with the state of Washington. After the decision was made to not force all the men and women whom I have launched in their own businesses to become my employees, I have decided to move to the state of Texas and continue on with my passion and vision to empower women in their own entrepreneurial endeavors.

I am confident after nearly 40 years of launching over 4,500 people (mainly moms and single moms) in their own entrepreneurial businesses that I have taken a new direction to empower women. I feel that we (as women) need to be healthy, fit and feel beautiful about ourselves in order to become successful. My hope is that in my final chapter of my life at age 57, I can not only participate and finish my first triathlon but also continue the last 40 years of helping others with however long I'm privileged to live on this planet through continuing to make a contribution.

My hero was and always will be my mother. Marie Mileti "Red" was the most loving and encouraging woman I have ever met. She died young in her early forties from heart disease but she inspired me so much because she really believed I could make a difference even though I lived in the NYC housing projects on welfare most of my young life. I lost her when I was 18 years old. She believed that I could become whatever I wanted to be and that I would make my way through life and make a positive difference on this planet. I feel I have a long way to go. But what a privilege to breathe the air and take each moment to make someone else's life better.

The words of encouragement that I would give to younger women are: never give up on your dreams. Even though life seems difficult at times, there is always a bright new story for you to participate in. And never, ever, forget to believe in yourself even if you are the only one who does. Always follow your heart. You have to live your own life and don't stop chasing the dream. Make your dreams your reality.

Photo by Gregory Paul

JEANNE BICE and ANGEL SMEDLEY

IN 1992, JEANNE BICE CREATED The Quacker Factory brand, which brings together designers and manufacturers of women's clothing. Headquartered in Boca Raton, Florida, it is a family-owned business. Jeanne's son, Tim Bice, is President and her daughter, Lee, is a designer and Creative Director. They are marketed primarily on QVC home shopping network and have a customer base exceeding three million women. The brand receives over 100 hours of national television each year and reaches an estimated 150 million viewers. They have the highest dollar-per-minute sales of any apparel brand sold on QVC.

The Quacker Factory fan base represents QVC's largest customer segment, "The Modern Heartland." As such, they are down-to-earth, fun-loving and giving women. The fans are called "Quackers," and many of them are teachers, care-givers and nurses and represent the "Real American Woman," the backbone of America.

Jeanne's philosophy is the key to their success: "Life's a journey, and we need to have fun along the way. Every woman needs a little sparkle and shine in her life. We make clothes that make people happy and give them the attention they deserve."

In February of 2010 Jeanne launched her "Moments to Remember" jewelry collection. It is sold on her website, www.quackerfactory.com and in various retail locations around the country. It is a variety of charms and signature bracelets.

Jeanne has authored three successful books in the last few years. Her latest, The Rubber Duck Principle, is currently sold on QVC and on her website. The Quacker Factory and Jeanne Bice have been featured in numerous national media outlets including The New York Times, The Washington Post, USA Today, Good Morning America, The View, Bonnie Hunt, Soup on E Entertainment and many others.

I was born in the small town of Fond du Lac, Wisconsin and went to college at the University of Wisconsin, Milwaukee where I vigorously pursued an "MRS" degree. Having always been self-motivated, I quickly succeeded in achieving this college goal. I married and moved with my new husband, Arlow Bice, to the even smaller town of Ripon, Wisconsin where we started a family.

My foray into teaching lower elementary classes was not as successful. It was much more fun planning and decorating the classroom than the actual teaching. Although I was successful, it was not what I wanted.

I had a son and daughter and set about the exciting business of being a mother and housewife. I loved all of my duties in these areas but it wasn't enough. I began crafting and taking cooking lessons, became a certified French chef, and enjoyed entertaining, shopping, traveling and generally expanding my horizons. I became a world-class shopper, exploring everything from the Sears catalog to Bloomingdale's, New York City. I entertained the world, heading up charity balls, tours of homes, traveling dinners and newcomer groups.

My husband Arlow owned the local radio station so I suggested I start a daily hour-long show looking at what was going on around town.

Thus began my first adventure into broadcasting with no inkling that some years down the road I would become something of a television personality.

I entered the retail business as a bored, rich housewife on Arlow's money and his suggestion. For so long I had been crafting and giving it all away, that Arlow felt it would be a great outlet for my talents. I went into business with a friend and opened a retail store called The Silent Woman, something of an ironic name, especially to those who knew me. We began to design clothes and added needlepoint pieces to them, and found out women bought clothes every day. So, we started designing clothes with appliqués on them, getting the look of needlepoint without all the work.

Soon people from Chicago who were vacationing in the area wanted The Silent Woman to wholesale for their retail shops. It started on a small scale. Then, one day my business partner said, "Let's go to the Chicago Apparel Mart and get a rep and start selling all over the country." We started with a long Santa skirt (I still have the original!). Two weeks later, Arlow called to say they had $150,000 worth of orders, but how were we going to make that happen? We formed a cottage industry with wonderful Wisconsin farm women and jumped into the wholesale business.

In 1981, Arlow and I scouted locations in Boca Raton, Florida for another retail shop. We signed the leases and found a place to live. Then tragically, at the young age of 42, Arlow dropped dead at my feet, leaving me a very poor widow before the move to Florida. All of my assets were tied up, and what I thought was there, what I thought I had…I didn't. What started as a plaything— something to occupy my time—became my job, my income, my lifeline! Coincidentally, around the same time, my partner divorced and found herself in much the same position. Now The Silent Woman had to support two families.

I moved to Florida and took on the task of running the Boca Raton store. Although my children had been left money in trust when Arlow died, they did not have access to it for many years and I was beyond broke. Grocery shopping with the change in the bottom of my purse was not uncommon. There were times when I was sure my next apartment would be a grocery cart under the Oakland Street Bridge. But,

I managed to work pretty much day and night to put both children through college until they came into their own money. After a few years of true struggling, my business partner became engaged and moved to London. Left on my own, I decided to close the two retail stores in order to stay focused on the wholesale end.

This forced me to focus solely on design. I spent the next 20 years honing my craft as one of the premiere designers of appliquéd, embroidered and embellished clothing, even working with other companies as their designer. I even went so far as to partner in a company with a man who left me holding the payroll one Friday afternoon with no money in the bank. He disappeared, and I was left to make that payroll good. Somehow, through sheer will and hard work, I managed to make that payroll but was forced to close the company. One of the men who worked there and I started a new company called JB Duckworth. We now had a factory with 120 sewers, and I was really in over my head.

After a year or so, I said to my son Tim, "This Duckworth is driving me Quackers! I should call it the Quacker Factory. And, I bet I could go to the flea market and sell this stuff, and I bet that the bottom line would be that I would make more money with a hell of a lot less stress." So, I made the rounds of flea markets through the country relying on the wrong men to help me through. It seemed that each decision I made was worse than the one before. I designed all the clothing by hand, got a few hours of sleep, and then designed the other side so I had product to sell under the name of JB Duckworth. This went on for years until Tim came into the business. He announced, "Mom, you'll be a little old lady with purple hair selling stuff on the street corner. We have to make life easier for you." I left the flea market screaming and crying because I had loved the personal contact with my customers.

So, with Tim by my side, in the early '90s, I started a label called The Quacker Factory and began to take notice of a new phenomenon known as home shopping. I began to watch a lot of television and got very excited about a network that called itself QVC. I felt like this would be the perfect forum for my whimsical and entertaining line of clothing. Plus, being the daughter of an auctioneer, I knew I would make a great guest.

How could I get in the front door? I went through my normal channels of having my sales reps make the approach and was greeted with little interest. Starting to get frustrated, I decided to put the project in God's hands. I made a big sign that said "QVC Yes!!!" and put it on the wall of my design studio.

Two weeks later I was contacted by the state of Florida's Department of Commerce saying that QVC was going to all 50 states looking for new entrepreneurs and would I like to participate in a big audition being held at the Tupperware Convention Center in Orlando the next month. As I filled out the application papers, the excitement began to build.

QVC was to begin their "50 in 50 Tour" in January of the following year and Florida was to be their fifth stop. I packed up a rack full of some of my favorite designs and headed to Orlando. QVC was seeing 300 vendors over two days and I was to be seen sometime on the second day. The vendors were each given a booth at the convention center and the buyers went up and down the aisles interviewing people and reviewing products. The buyers would select 20 to appear on a three hour show on the first Saturday in February.

The day wore on and no one had visited my booth. We broke for lunch and still no visit from the buyer. The day drew near to a close and still nothing. It began to look very bleak indeed, but I knew that if I could get just five minutes I could win them over. Finally at the very end of the day The Quacker Factory was seen by a buyer and was the last product to be reviewed.

A week or so passed before I finally heard that I had been selected to appear. On February 4, 1995 Jeanne Bice and The Quacker Factory made the QVC debut. Mine was the final product of the three hour show and it sold out from previews before it even got on the air. The rest, as they say, is history.

Since that time many amazing things have happened for Quacker Factory. My line of clothing has expanded from one cow and one cat shirt to hundreds of new designs for the Quacker and "peeper" alike. My two books have led to appearances on Good Morning America, CBS's The Early Show, The Tony Danza Show and two separate appearances on The View. My days are filled with visions of Quackers dancing in my head…there is always something brewing at Quacker Factory! I'm very excited about my QVC success and I'm looking forward to the awesome things that are yet to come.

My mother and father were my inspiration. They both loved the challenge of the business world. They came from nothing and retired to Florida at the age of 50 and lived comfortably until they were 95. My dad and mom gave their children "wings" to fly through their own example. My other inspiration was Sr. Michaela. She was my favorite teacher in high school. She saw talent in a very chubby girl with a big mouth. She told me, "Jeanne, you are a Star. Shine Bright" and it gave me the courage to do just that!

My best advice is that you can be or do anything if you just believe you can. I have a sign over my bed. It hangs flat on my bedroom ceiling and says: "The Secret of having it all is Believing you do." Success in life has nothing to do with talent, education, looks or money; it has to do with what you believe. Henry Ford said it best: "If you think you can…you can. If you think you can't…then you can't." It's So Easy—Believe You Can.

Post Script by Angel Smedley

Our beloved Jeanne Bice passed away on June 10, 2011. It was a terrible loss to us all, she loved life and often said, "Life's a Party. Celebrate every day!!" She lived what she spoke!!!

I am honored to continue her legacy by being the on air spokesperson for the Quacker Factory. I have over 25 years of experience in the fashion industry, and now I am going on five years as the on air representative for Quacker. Jeanne was my "fairy Godmother." She was always there to offer me advice, and also to offer me several jobs within her company. She was like a second mother to me and had to fight for me to be in the position I currently hold. She saw something in me, she knew I'd be right for the part, and she fought for what she believed in. I thank her every day! My mentor, my friend, my fairy Godmother! And inspiration to me and to so many others, and she, as she would put it—"was just a fat farm girl from Wisconsin."

Angel Smedley

M Y STORY BEGINS ALL THE way back in high school. I did not join many activities in high school, but I did join the modeling club. I wanted to model and this was the best way for me to learn how to walk, how to apply makeup, and also learn routines that we performed in our annual shows. Of course, I got a ton of push back due the fact that I am a full figured girl. But I enjoyed it and still kept hope of following this career path at some point. I attended college and performed in plays and musicals, still with modeling always on my mind. While in school, I worked in a retail store and always heard ladies telling me—oh you have such a pretty face, you should model. While attending a professional dinner (after graduation I was in the communications field), I met a woman who was an actress and model and she asked me, "So Angel, what do you want to do?" And I replied, "I want to pursue plus size modeling." Funny thing is, she had a friend who needed a plus model for a bridal show. I went and auditioned for that show and got it—my first paid job!! And there I met Trudy, who was modeling at QVC and gave me the person to contact to start modeling there. Things were a lot different back in 1991, but the producer met me and said, "Great, I will call you when we need you." Several months later, I had a friend take some photos of me, and I took these photos to my first agency: Askins Models in Philadelphia. And that is how my career began.

Things just went up from here. I have modeled on TV shows, QVC, and on the runways around Philadelphia and Washington, DC. I have been hired to commentate and coordinate fashion shows and style fashion shows. I was even hired to be a traveling fashion editor for a plus size fashion magazine, a fit model, and now finally a Brand Ambassador for the Quacker Factory on QVC.

There have been many hurdles in my career, but I just keep flying over them! Everyone has struggles, so I feel that it is extremely important to FEED YOUR BRAIN with positive things every day! Tell yourself you are worthy, tell yourself you are successful, tell yourself YOU DESERVE great things! Sometimes in the fast-paced world that we all currently enjoy, I even forget to do this, but recently I realized that I must NEVER forget to do these things. The world can be a negative place, and I can choose to be a positive force or a negative one. I always choose to be a positive force!

JILL HOLTERMANN BOWERS

CLAUS HOLTERMANN, THE FOUNDER OF Holtermann's Bakery, was born in Hanover, Germany. As a new immigrant to America, Claus began working at the Frederick Engler Bakery in New York. In 1882, Claus relocated to Richmond, Staten Island where he bought the Garret Homan Bakery on Center Street. Claus, along with his family, lived in a home he built himself in the rectory of what is now St. Patrick's Church. In 1907 Claus passed away leaving his four sons to run the Garret Homan Bakery. In 1930 the four Holtermann sons sold the bakery to Hathaway Bakery.

Albert Holtermann, the youngest of the four sons, decided in 1930 that he would continue his family craftsmanship as a baker in his own establishment known as Holtermann's Bakery. Along with the support of his wife Dorothy, the bakery was custom built on Arthur Kill Road.

Through the decades the bakery has remained in its original location on Arthur Kill Road while evolving from the days of horse and buggy delivery and our famous orange Difco home delivery truck of the 1950s. Within the past decade we have been featured on On the Road with Al Roker, in the culinary magazine Cooks Illustrated and a PBS special on New York's Oldest Family Owned Establishments. While time has passed, Holtermann's still strives to meet the demands and expectations of our loyal customer base. We have maintained strong community ties while receiving the honor of having our cakes served at birthdays, graduations, meetings, bereavements and other family events.

As a native Staten Islander, I have been very lucky and fortunate to have spent my years living in the tight- knit community known as Richmondtown. We lived in a cute small house with my three brothers Cliff, Craig and Jeff, and my two sisters Wendy and Brenda. I have fond memories of visiting my family members who all lived within a five-block radius of each other. Many warm sunny days were spent riding my bike to Eger's Nursing Home as a candy striper or even to my aunt's to play dominoes and bake pies.

As a teenager, I found myself active in our family business, Holtermann's Bakery. The bakery has been the setting of many formative experiences throughout my life. As a young, impressionable woman I watched strong Holtermann women manage the front end of the bakery which was our retail store. My friendly mother greeted customers with a smile and chatted with each one of them about what was occurring in their families' lives. My grandmother held the utmost respect for our customers, instilling in all of us the motto "The customer is always right." We always lived up to that standard.

Times change, as they always do, and I married my high school sweetheart, Bob. Bob and I have spent years going through good times and passing through tough times as all married couples do. We take pride in our family: our daughter Kristin, son Robert, granddaughter Hailey, and son-in-law Patrick. While Bob has passed on his love of cars to Robert, I have been active in the Girl Scouts with my daughter Kristen for the past 27 years.

My involvement with the Girl Scouts still continues today as I attempt to strengthen young women to become strong independent women of society. I feel such a strong sense of pride and accomplishment when I witness my Girl Scouts achieve the highest possible award in scouting, The Gold Award, for displaying the leadership skills necessary in the professional world.

Throughout my days, my role of Girl Scout leader, Service Unit Manager for 1200 girls, and Program Manager for Staten Island, became interwoven. I have brought my love of baking to the Girl Scouts, introducing the concept of creativity and independent baking. Continuing to educate the younger generation of Staten Islanders about the history of my family business has been a goal and a great experience of mine. Currently, the Girl Scouts have been associating with the New York State Professional Women's Association, correlating with a board member on a survey along with Wagner College, The College of Staten Island, and St. John's University. This survey displays the positive and independent characteristics of the new workforce.

As the present meets the future combining the history of my family bakery along with the optimistic attitude of the young women of the workforce remain a top priority of mine. Historic Richmondtown, which has been a presence in Staten Island for hundreds of years, will also be a moving force in the future. I have always considered Richmondtown to be the original home of the Holtermann's Bakery. By exposing the youth of Staten Island to Richmondtown, I feel that they too are learning about one of Staten Island's treasures.

The heroes of my lifetime are my grandparents. My first impression was in the second grade when our class trip went to Holtermann's Bakery. When the class came to meet my family, my grandma greeted us at the door. She welcomed all the children and gave us a tour of the bakery. I watched my Uncle Al and Grandpa making pies, cake decorating and icing cakes. My dad fried donuts. Each one of my classmates received a powdered cake donut that we all ate and enjoyed.

I learned about hard work and dedication over the years. While in high school, I started working at the bakery part-time. At that time we had 24 delivery routes and my job was to make boxes and ice cakes. Uncle Al would say, "While you're icing cakes, your mind should be thinking of what you're going to do next." He would say, "Time is money" and the only way to make pies was "his" way. I worked close to my grandma and she was always pleasant and thoughtful. She greeted her customers and knew them all by name.

My grandpa was 6 feet 5 inches tall. He was a hard worker, always giving all of his life to make the bakery continue. I have worked with my mom and dad for many years. Our customers appreciated our responsible management skills, leadership and most of all, our caring conversation and organization. As for dear Dad, well, where do I begin? Dad has worked in the bakery for 65 years. Over the years he's taught me how to manage the bakery while keeping the customers happy. Trying to accommodate them while exceeding above their expectations. It is the hard work, time, dedication and love, but most of all the heart of my family name of Holtermann's that keeps me going.

When I'm not attending meetings for Girl Scouts, the bakery or The Business and Professional Women's Club of Staten Island, I'm spending quality time with Hailey reading or strolling along. I enjoy spending the day shopping with Kristin. We go everywhere together. She's always supporting my volunteer events. If I'm not having dinner with my friends and family, I'm busy at Richmondtown with my mom. She is always volunteering and I'm following in her footsteps. My son Robert is a shopper too. For all the craziness in my life I thank my family and friends for all of their support.

My future endeavor is to provide a tour through Richmondtown where it all began. People of all ages can be educated in the Holtermann history. People can learn the art of being creative and having fun with food. I would like to show them a step by step technique to make pies. My motto will be: "Everyone bake 'til your heart's content!"

photo by Tommy MacGregor

JULIE DEFRUSCIO

JULIE DEFRUSCIO IS THE MOTHER of three children, all with type I diabetes. Along with her friend and business partner, Dawn Juneau, she is the Co-Owner of Pump Wear Inc. (www.pumpwearinc.com). In 2008 Julie and Dawn took their company a step further and branched out with a new company called Girly Girl Studio, (www.girlygirlstudio.com) a place where you can design your own handbag.

Julie holds a bachelor'sdegree in Business Administration and has over 30 years of experience in corporate America. She has served as Chair for the Business Council of Cohoes, and as a Board member for JDRF, the Albany Colonie Chamber. Julie has also been a Co-Leader for the Girl Scouts and past PTA President.

I started my career in corporate America at the age of 18 with GMAC. I worked with them for 24 years, until the ultimate downsizing seized us all. I then went to work for five years with TD Banknorth; another opportunity where I perfected my selling skills and techniques. During my years with GMAC, my daughter Nikki Tyler Defruscio (who at the time was two years old) was diagnosed with juvenile type I diabetes. At the time I didn't realize just how this would really change my life. She was diagnosed on June 19, 2000. This date will be planted in our minds forever. You see, that's the day that our lives and Nikki Tyler's life changed forever.

The best way to describe our life with diabetes would be one big roller coaster. We were constantly chasing highs and lows, forever trying to figure out when the insulin would peak and always trying to predict what the unpredictable Nikki Tyler would want to eat! As most who have small children would agree, this was not an easy task. Meals became a battleground where we knew that we had to get Nikki to eat something. Often we would have to settle for Cheetos since the insulin was going to peak and she would get too low and Cheetos were the only thing that she would eat. Our lives were on hold and everything revolved around handling the high or low of the moment.

Through all of this we searched out websites for information and went to support groups to gain support and knowledge of some way to help our daughter. The common theme that emerged was that the children on the insulin pump seemed to be getting better numbers, more control and enjoyed happier times.

Finding a doctor willing to put a then three-year-old on the insulin pump was also a struggle. Thankfully for Nikki Tyler and our family we found a wonderful doctor, Dr. Jill Abelseth, and her nurse, RN diabetes educator Eileen Hogan. They were willing to help us gain control over this monster of an illness. They understood our need to bring Nikki Tyler's blood sugars into line. Because of Nikki Tyler's uncontrollable diabetes, she was very moody and we wanted our happy and fun-loving little girl back. Looking back on just how out of control her numbers were, I can now understand just how sick Nikki Tyler really was and that the mood swings were a direct result of her inability to maintain a balanced blood sugar level.

A major reason for choosing insulin pump therapy for Nikki Tyler was to gain better control of her diabetes and to hopefully avoid future complications that are too heartbreaking to even think about. The first three months of putting Nikki on the pump were very emotional for me. It was hard seeing our beautiful little girl wearing this pump that was her life support. Also with the insulin pump came a different problem: the pump is the size of a beeper and holds a vial of insulin that is dispensed throughout the day. Where do you put this on a small child? If we clipped it on Nikki's pants it would pull them down...and the holder that came with the pump was very "medical-looking." That's when I started to purchase t-shirts for Nikki and had pockets sewn on the back for her. They looked really cute, Nikki liked wearing them and I had easy access to the pump.

One night my best friend Dawn and I started to search for other items that might be used to give Nikki different ways of wearing her pump. We quickly discovered that our choices were limited. It was at that time we decided that it didn't have to be this way. Children and adults should have fun and creative ways to wear the insulin pump. Dawn and I had always thought we would do a business together, we just never thought that it would develop from our love for Nikki and the thousands of other children and adults that suffer from this illness. We created Pump Wear Inc., (www.pumpwearinc.com) a website that offers children and adults fun and creative ways to wear the insulin pump along with "cure diabetes" support items. Pump Wear Inc. is committed to making a difference in the lives of people with diabetes. Both Dawn's family and mine help in coming up with ideas for the designs and everyone helps with folding brochures, stuffing envelopes and filling orders. Dawn's girls and my sons even help us out when we do a show. Thankfully we both have husbands who have given us their support on our new adventure so Pump Wear Inc. has truly become a family affair.

Today Nikki Tyler is a happy and fun-loving little girl who is getting ready to start kindergarten. Maintaining her blood sugar level is still a struggle but the insulin pump has allowed us the flexibility we thought we had lost and the ability to treat high blood sugar levels quickly while minimizing lows. The insulin pump is not the "cure" but a way to give our daughter the best chance at maintaining her blood sugar levels.

Nikki Tyler has now been on the pump for over a year. I look back and know that we made the right decision for our daughter.

Food is no longer an issue. I never thought that we would gain so much pleasure in being able to tell our daughter "Yes, Nikki you can have the chocolate donut." We have been given back our life and the lives of our two sons. There were so many times when either my husband or I couldn't go to a baseball game because one of us would have to stay home with Nikki. I think that this bothered me the most about diabetes: it's a family illness and we were losing precious time with our sons because there was always something going on with Nikki.

The pump has given us back our freedom and allowed us to function as a family again. Now Nikki can sleep in the morning! She can eat lunch at the same time as everyone else! We don't have to be home at a certain time so that she can get her insulin and eat. When we have a high we can gain control of it so much quicker. Now we feel like we are in control! We still have our ups and downs but we have better numbers, more control and definitely more freedom in our lives. We know that with Nikki on the pump we are giving her the best chance there is for controlling her diabetes. By being allowed to put her on the pump at the age of three we feel like we are saving Nikki from years of out of control blood sugars and the devastation that this can cause to her body. The pump is not a cure for juvenile diabetes but it has given us hope!

Since Nikki Tyler's diagnosis our two sons have also been diagnosed. We live life to the fullest and try to teach our children how to work around the numbers.

My hero growing up was Lucille Ball. I was so amazed by her ability to laugh and make others laugh. She was a great lady that accomplished so much, took risks and always had a positive attitude. I still love watching her shows. One of the things that truly inspired me about Ms. Ball was the fact that she had good business sense in running her studio and her many other endeavors. She was and still is my hero.

We continue to grow and strive to make a difference. We are passionate about what we do, so even though the hours are long and running a company can be stressful we love it! When you are passionate about something, somehow it's not work! My advice to young women is if you have a passion for something, then go for it! Prepare your life around the things that you are passionate about. As we go through life it is so nice to go to work every day if you are passionate about what you do. So if you like fashion, prepare your goals and life around fashion. I never knew what I was really passionate about until I was in my thirties and my daughter was diagnosed with type I diabetes. That's when I found my passion for providing products for children and adults who have type I diabetes. I thrive on building our company because it has my heart and soul! Don't settle for less!

LIZ LANGE

L IZ LANGE, FOUNDER AND CREATIVE Director of Liz Lange Maternity, is a fashion and retail pioneer. Armed with the philosophy that women should look and feel beautiful during pregnancy, she has single-handedly revolutionized maternity style and society's perception of pregnant women in just 10 short years.

Lange's path to success was based on her entrepreneurial instinct and her fashion industry experience. She graduated from Brown University in 1988, and worked afterwards at both Vogue magazine and a small design firm in New York City. It was at the design firm where Lange first developed the idea for a sophisticated chic and slim fitting collection of maternity clothing.

The fitted maternity silhouette became Lange's calling card. This innovative design approach quickly attracted celebrities, fashion insiders, businesswomen and stay-at-home moms and moms-to-be to her small shop on Lexington Avenue. The word-of-mouth effect was bolstered by key press features in publications like The New York Times, In Style and Oprah magazine that hailed Lange as a fashion trailblazer.

Lange's business grew to three Liz Lange Maternity flagship boutiques. Her secondary line, Liz Lange for Target is the exclusive maternity clothing offered at all Target stores and on Target.com. She is the only maternity designer to have shown her work at New York's Fashion Week, and the only maternity designer to be a member of the prestigious Council of Fashion Designers of America.

Lange's achievements and swift expansion quickly drew the attention of major retailers. In 2001, Nike approached Lange to create the Liz Lange for Nike line of maternity active wear to be sold in Lange's boutiques and through Nike's retail channels. She has also enjoyed partnerships with Nikon cameras and the Bliss Spas, owned by Starwood Hotels.

She is the author of Liz Lange's Maternity Style: How to look Fabulous during the Most Fashion-Challenged Time. She currently is at work on her follow-up book, The Fourth Trimester.

Liz Lange's accomplishments have not only been praised by the fashion community, but by the business community as well. Her work has been covered by Crain's New York, Entrepreneur magazine, Women's Wear Daily, Harvard Business Review and Fortune, who named her a "Top 10 to Watch" entrepreneur. Most recently, she was named to Crain's New York's highly prestigious annual "40 under 40" list. When she sold her business in the fall of 2007 it was reported in Women's Wear Daily and the Wall Street Journal as a $50 million transaction.

Lange is a member of the Committee of 200 and a board member of Fertile Hope. Additionally she is a sought-after speaker, and is actively involved in many charities in her hometown of New York City where she lives with her husband, Jeffrey Lange, and their children Gus, 9 and Alice, 7.

Liz's business has been featured in Women's Wear Daily (March 2005), Harvard Business Review (January 2005), Working Mother (November 2004), Entrepreneur (June 2004), Crain's New York (June 2004, August 2001), Time Style and Design (Spring 2004), Fortune (September 2003), Entrepreneur (November 2001) and Women's Wear Daily (August 2001). Liz was a Master Award Honoree at the NAWBO

Signature Awards in 2007 and was named to Working Mother Magazine's "Top 25 Working Mothers List" in 2004. She was a finalist in Ernst & Young's Entrepreneur of the Year Awards in 2003, and was named one of Fortune magazine's "Top 10 Entrepreneurs to Watch" in 2003.

———◆———

My idea for my maternity wear line began while I was working at Vogue as a writer. It was there I fell in love with fashion. When I left Vogue, I met a young designer and apprenticed for him, which was like a crash-course in fashion.

Then I married, and found that my friends (who were in their early thirties) would complain that they couldn't find maternity clothes that looked good. They would come to buy material wholesale and inevitably the clothes looked like oversized huge tents. That's when my "Ah-ha!" moment came. Stretch fabric was new to the market place. I believed clothes that were loose only made people look larger…so stretch fabric that was fitted actually made you look skinnier.

Once I made this realization, I just knew it would be a success. I started my own line in November of 1997 and worked on it for eight months. Although I was plagued with self-doubt, I persevered, although none of my friends thought it was a great idea. As my business grew, I learned how important it is to stay in close contact with my customers. To this day, I believe in answering my own e-mails.

My world changed when at the young age of 35 with two small children, I received the phone call that no woman ever wants to get—it was my gynecologist delivering the devastating news that I had cervical cancer. I had always worn many hats: I went into "take- charge" mode. I decided on a hysterectomy, followed by chemotherapy and radiation treatments. I've always been a private person and wanted to keep my battle private as well. However, now eight years later and cancer free, I am a proud spokeswoman for the Gynecological Cancer Foundation. The message is loud and clear: the need for women to get regular pap tests is crucial.

I was a bit of a bookworm growing up. I had no idea that I would be an entrepreneur. I thought I was going to be a writer! I worshiped and even wrote to many of my favorite authors: Judy Blume, Madeline L'Engle, Roald Dahl and Jane Austin. I identified with Elizabeth Bennett in Pride and Prejudice and loved C.S. Lewis.

I think reading is a great way to find your own voice. Hearing how others express themselves is a great way to learn. Remember that you can accomplish anything. Listen to Helen Reddy's song "I Am Woman" whenever you feel in doubt, I still do. Don't let anyone tell you that you can't do something.

LORI DENNIS

LORI DENNIS GRADUATED FROM THE UCLA Interior Architecture and Design Program where she currently serves on the Alumni Association Board. While completing her coursework Lori was an in-house designer for SeminarPlanet.com. In 1999, she went to work for Cheryl Rowley Interior Design. A year later she established her own firm, Dennis Design Group.

Lori has been published in countless magazines throughout the world and appears on several television programs. An expert in sustainable design, Lori has lectured on the topic for UCLA and the California State University Interior Design Programs. She's also a recurring guest on HGTV's XM Radio with Nancy Glass and KABC Talk Radio. She passed the NCIDQ in 2006 and the LEED certification exam in 2007.

I was born to a young hippie in 1969. She divorced my father when I was an infant and I never saw or heard from him again. My mom was immature, wild, selfish, lazy, violent and poor during the early 1970s. She left her family and support system in New York and headed for San Diego, California. My mother and I hitchhiked across the country with a Hefty bag of our belongings and not one cent. Truck drivers gave us rides and bought us food and hotel rooms. To this day when I see a truck driver, I believe they are the angels of the highway. This was the beginning of a lot of moving. By the time I graduated from high school I had gone to 24 different schools.

At this point in the early 1970s, my mom was on husband number two and they were both drugged out and violent. She partied like a rock star for years. I was more like a neglected puppy in the background than a woman's child. When she did pay attention to me, it was often to hit me because I was annoying her. I went to bed hungry on my Salvation Army cot many nights.

As a little girl I spent a lot of time by myself. Things went on this way until my sister was born when I was four. I then became like a mother to her, feeding her what little food we had, bathing, dressing, teaching and protecting her. When I was eight, my mother was on husband number three and had given birth to my little brother. The burden to excel in school, sports, dance, maintain a social life and raise two babies took a toll on a third grader. The neglect, verbal and physical abuse continued, but this third husband was a responsible guy, so we weren't starving anymore.

Then, she divorced him and married a mad scientist, who made tiles for the space shuttle program and sold pounds of marijuana. By this time I was in middle school and I knew enough to start complaining to school officials about her behavior. The police showed up a few times and I eventually wound up being allowed to move back to the East Coast to live with her sister (my aunt) and her husband.

Understandably I had emotional problems at this time, suffering from shame and embarrassment about who I was and where I had come from. I lied a lot and my aunt and uncle seemed to always be angry with me, saying, "You are just like your mom." I never really felt welcome in their home as a teenager, even though I was grateful.

Although I was angry and sad as a child, something inside of me said, "Hold on, Lori. One day you will be in charge and your life will be good. Do your best to survive and succeed and you will be ok." My way of coping was to control the things I could at the time. I tried very hard in school, achieving straight As. I excelled in after-school sports and other programs. I belonged to social groups. I guess I was lucky because I was smart, pretty and people seemed to be attracted to me, but I still felt completely robbed of my childhood, and on top of it all, insecure.

I continued to stay positive and tried as hard as I could. Time passed. I was admitted to UCLA for an undergraduate and a master's degree. Now, I own a successful interior design firm, I have the most wonderful husband who I love dearly and my children are on their way. I realized I could forgive all of the people who raised me. I accepted that just because someone is an adult doesn't mean they know the right way to behave. I have healed and have a good relationship with everyone in my family.

I would tell today's young girls to never quit trying to be your best. When the people around you fail as role models, look to your teachers in school, coaches, clergy, friends, sports figures and librarians. And read. It makes you aware of things you never knew and provides ideas and options for your personal success.

If your home life is shaky, stay away as long as possible—go to the library, after-school programs and friends' homes. Volunteer to help kids who are less fortunate than you, maybe be a big sister at school and help a younger kid read. This empowers you. Stay away from the kids who get into trouble, who smoke cigarettes, do drugs and have sex. Keep your self-respect intact and believe that you have worth. That magic day comes when you are 18 and you are free. Make sure you have set yourself up to succeed when you are ready to go out into the world on your own. Remember you are a beautiful creature and there is a world out there waiting for you to shine.

LUCIA BURNS (AKA LUCIA RAMAZETTI ON YOUTUBE)

M Y STORY IS ABOUT HAVING PLANS. No plans and many plans all converging at once. I have invented two products; one is for luggage ID and one is more like a trophy for personal empowerment.

I've learned this about life; you can start over for two reasons— because you *have to* or because you *want to*—and sometimes for *both* reasons. I grew up the youngest of four children. My mother left an abusive marriage when I was six years old. She sold everything we owned and we boarded a bus from Michigan to California. We moved from here to there and by eighth grade I had gone to seven different schools spread over five cities and three states. Each new school was an opportunity to make new friends and pursue new interests and *start over.*

I really didn't think about my future in a strategic way since I had no control over anything. As the youngest child, my voice had the least impact so I learned to just roll with the changes and situations. My easygoing attitude was beneficial under those circumstances but little did I know I was missing a major component to living a successful life.

When I was eleven I wanted to be like Carol Burnett. I loved her show and she was so funny. I didn't have a single thought about how to actually *become* a comedian; I just wanted to *be* one. At sixteen, I did make one long term plan. I decided at some point in my 40's I would cut my long brown hair into a chin length bob. This was my life plan...all of it. (Pause and plan your better future here.) Side note: I did bob my hair when I turned 44. I thought I should honor that commitment. It was truly pitiful . . . not a good look for me.

After high school, I went to community college for two years and it was only then that I realized I needed to begin to think about my future. I had been studying art since it fit my natural talents but I found that I really loved psychology! I decided to transfer to a university and I would pursue that as a career. Finally I had a plan!

Then without warning, my 22-year-old sister Elizabeth committed suicide in front of my brother. Within six months, everything that was working fell apart. I developed a crippling fear of flying. My relationship with my mother became suddenly miserable. She quickly remarried and I had to move out on my own. I was totally unprepared! Needless to say, I didn't get to the university, instead I was 19 working two jobs to get by and felt utterly adrift.

Life was so random and unmanageable that I reverted back to living for the day without any direction or plans for my future. I ended up married at 24 and then divorced at 38 with two kids. After the divorce I had to figure out how to provide for my two boys. I was blessed to have truly incredible sons who make me proud every day and I was determined not to let them down.

I knew they were watching me and learning from everything I did.

I had my real estate license so I went full on into the business. That was working for me but I was still praying for an opportunity to express myself at another level.

As I was determined to finally overcome my fear of flying (another important demonstration for my sons) I had planned a trip to NY to visit relatives. I bought cheap black luggage for the trip and was immediately aware that I could barely recognize it in my own home let alone at an airport buried with other black bags. So I thought it would be nice if there were a BIG bright band that I could put around the bags so I could spot them instantly. I went to the Internet but couldn't find anything like what I was looking for. So I made a few for our trip and that was it! As soon as our bags came down the chute at JFK I yelled out "Look! There's our bag!" (But inside I was thinking "Hey I'm still alive!) Immediately people started asking me where I got those great ID bands and where could they get one.

So I decided to start over...I had to! I couldn't let this chance go by. Just like that, Luggage Huggers were born. They are wide bright, colored and/or patterned spandex bands that fit the middle of your suitcase like a tube top. The patterns are unlimited and if you put the same band on all your mismatched bags, then instantly you have matching luggage. And you really can spot them from across an airport! They are also great sellers for corporate groups when they get branded with logos. Luggage Huggers were an original idea that I had to pursue with commitment. They became my spandex baby. I had no other source of income after the real estate market crashed in 2007 so I really did worry about going out on a limb and becoming an entrepreneur. What if I failed...in front of my kids!?

In my life of fresh starts, what was one more life-altering, spine-tingling attempt at having it all? So I did it. Now I am enjoying the rewards of inventing my life on my terms. Luggage Huggers are sold in national travel catalogs and retailers as well as through my website. My sons have been taught to plan for their success and it gives me immense pleasure to talk with them about their plans and goals. They have definitely gained knowledge from my experience!

Then something else happened. Something BIG!

I have met and mentored many women on their journeys. Some are starting their own businesses and I offer as much advice and support as I can. Others are overcoming a divorce and looking for their fresh start.

Some just need to learn to own their power and recognize their potential. And in this process I have been in the path of women who had "them" and women who need "them."

Yes, I am taking about having balls! Let's face it ladies, today '*a girls gotta have balls.*' She-BALLS to be exact! As a joke I made a pair of She-BALLS for a girlfriend who is a self-made millionaire and was in the early stages of starting another business. I made a pair of balls for her to demonstrate in physical form just what an amazing powerful leader she is. I crafted them from deflated silver balloons attached to a silver cord and tied them with a pink bow. Oh, and sprinkled them with crystals so they are shiny and beautiful yet still a symbol of power! I gave them to her for her birthday and when she lifted her balls out of the bag the room erupted!

Next thing you know, I have Balls of Steel, Brass Balls, Lady Balls, Grow A Pair, etc., blinged out t-shirts, hats, and it will go on! She-BALLS can be sent like you would send flowers for any occasion, only these last ways longer and are truly that shot in the arm when you need to bring up your masculine energy! They are delivered in a lovely ribbon-tied gift box with a display stand to hang the delicate She-BALLS and your personal note of encouragement or congratulations. An outward symbol of an inner emotion that empowers you and energizes you at a glance!

I have a website for that too! The message around the meaning of She-BALLS is what truly powers my day.

I have earned my balls many times over, but I still felt like a fraud. I was speaking to some ladies about empowerment when I was struck with the contradiction that I am promising to them that *they* possess the power to become and overcome anything. Yet *I* had never had the balls to face my earliest, scariest, most secret, longest held desire. I had no business telling anyone else to do more than I am willing to do myself.

So I did it! It really was the biggest thing I had ever *chosen* to do in my life! I took a few classes, wrote six minutes of original material, took the stage at a crowded comedy club in downtown Scottsdale and did a standup routine. And I killed! (that's good in comedy speak) My six minutes of fame lives on YouTube forever and while I could probably improve, the fact that I didn't just pass out or stand there is a victory on its own!

The circle was closed. I was braver than I thought I could be. I dared do the thing I feared the most. I have She-BALLS and as my shirts say "BRING IT ON!"

I've learned this about life too; never ever believe that your past is the limit of your future. We are all put into circumstances that we did not choose or cannot control. These experiences leave a print on you but are not a blueprint for your future. There are so many people with great stories of achievement, who at some point in their lives said "ENOUGH!" and took control by deciding that they not only wanted better, but that they deserved better.

Once you decide to have it better, you must figure out what "better" means to you. Define it so that you recognize it when you see it and you will know how to behave in accordance with what you want to achieve. Celebrate yourself with a kind and loving inner dialog for each step you take in the right direction, for each correct decision, and you will get addicted to feeling proud of yourself. Before you know it, you will be operating on a different level than just a month before. Good choices will come easier and opportunities will show up where there was nothing but nothing before.

Grab your She-Balls and get out there and don't let another day go by where you are waiting to take the stage of your life. ENOUGH!

MELLODY HOBSON

MELLODY HOBSON IS PRESIDENT OF Ariel Investments, a Chicago-based money management firm that serves retirement plans and individual investors through its no-load mutual funds and manages separate accounts for institutional clients. As President, Mellody is responsible for firm-wide management and strategic planning, overseeing all operations outside of research and portfolio management. Additionally, she serves as Chairman of the Board of Trustees for Ariel Investment Trust. She joined the company in 1991 after graduating from Princeton University where she received her degree from the Woodrow Wilson School of International Relations and Public Policy. Mellody has become a nationally recognized voice on financial literacy and investor education. She is a spokesperson for both the annual Ariel/Schwab Black Investor Survey and the 2009 Ariel/Hewitt study, "401(k) Plans in Living Color." She is also actively involved with a variety of civic and professional institutions. Her community outreach includes serving as a Board member of the Chicago Public Library and its foundation, The Field Museum, The Chicago Public Education Fund and The Sundance Institute. She is also a director of three public companies: DreamWorks Animation SKG, Inc., The Estée Lauder Companies Inc. and Starbucks Corporation. Additionally, she is on the Board of Governors of the Investment Company Institute and is a member of the SEC Investment Advisory Committee. She is also a former trustee of Princeton University. Mellody is a member of the Economic Club of Chicago, the Commercial Club of Chicago, the Young Presidents' Organization (YPO) and is a Henry Crown Fellow of the Aspen Institute.224

Mellody has been a featured guest on ABC's Nightline and World News Tonight. In 2007, she became a regular columnist in Black Enterprise and is frequently quoted in various news publications such as Money, Fortune, Pensions & Investments, Business Week and The Wall Street Journal. For more information on Mellody's business, visit www.arielinvestments.com. My heroes are the people closest to me; specifically, my mother, teachers and friends. For young girls today who are searching to find their voice, I borrow a quote from Judy Collins: "As women we are raised to have rescue fantasies but I am here to tell you, no one is coming." It's important to add that as women, we can rescue ourselves. To me this means living my own life and not the life that someone else envisions for me.

photo by Ben Asen Photography

NANCE L. SCHICK, ESQ.

NANCE L. SCHICK, ESQ. IS A counselor at law, business and conflict resolution. She earned her Juris Doctor from the State University of New York at Buffalo and her Bachelor of Science in Sports Administration from the University of Louisville. Non-traditional routes to success are her specialty. She advises actors, authors, construction contractors, designers, fitness and yoga instructors, film and stage producers, models and other small businesses on a variety of operational issues. She also defends employers of all sizes in workers' compensation claims. She has worked as a minor league hockey agent, a small-market model, an adaptive apparel designer, a fitness instructor, a sports marketer and a professional sports team mascot.

Nance has negotiated minor league player contracts for teams and players, lending her insight regarding the interests of both parties and the negotiable non- monetary compensation involved. She has helped her clients with branding, business formation, business planning, contracts, marketing and publicity. She takes their successes personally and works tirelessly to help them achieve beyond their expectations. Nance L. Schick is an unconventional attorney, even in New York City. As the sole proprietor of the law firm that carries her name, she represents businesses of all sizes in their "people- related" issues. From forming strategic partnerships to resolving litigation, she recognizes that most clients seek legal counsel when they are in fear and she tries to empower them so they can make the best decisions under the circumstances. "There will always be conflict," she says. "My clients are getting better at resolving theirs all of the time. So am I!"

As an athlete, Nance maintains a training regimen that includes weight training, spinning, running, yoga, hiking, walking and playing kickball. She played third base at the University of Kentucky and tried out for the 1996 United States Olympic softball team. She has also experimented with Pilates, tai chi, figure skating, inline skating, rock climbing, whitewater rafting, skiing, basketball, volleyball and tag football. For more information on Nance L Schick and her law practice, please visit her website at www.nschicklaw.com.

———◆———

I know conflict. My career and life have been full of start-ups and setbacks. It took six years to complete my undergraduate degree, often taking time off because my mom was being treated for cancer and my nephew needed a stable home. I paid my way through school by working multiple concurrent jobs. I worked in third-shift operations management at United Parcel Service, going into work around 11 p.m. and getting home around 6 a.m., when I would have "breakfast" with my mother and nephew. During some semesters, I'd go directly to early morning classes. Other times, I'd try to nap before afternoon classes, hoping I could drag myself out of a deep sleep when the alarm went off. After classes, I would go to a second job as a waitress, freelance writer, fitness instructor, high school softball coach or trade show model. I don't know when I actually slept for full eight hour shifts. My nephew would often wake me because his mom just wasn't ready to be a mom and he could never awaken her as easily as he could me. He would patter into my room and hold my eyelids open, saying "Natz, you 'wake?" I always got up.

I finally finished my degree the same year my mom had a lung removed. The breast cancer had metastasized and flowed to her lung. Her doctors told me to prepare for the worst. We did not expect her to live through the year. During the same time period, my sister had moved in with a man who got her high and beat her. My nephew sometimes called and begged, "Come get me." It seems I was always taking care of him or my mom, but I wouldn't have it any other way. My degree waited, and I still see it as one of my greatest achievements.

I still get teary-eyed when I think about the Christmas in which my mother gave me a framed copy of my bachelor's degree certificate. I had moved to Texas before I could pick it up, and I assumed that after a year, it had been destroyed. But the University of Louisville went above and beyond and helped my mother get it. With one lung and a weakened body, she trekked across the cold windy campus to give me a gift I will always appreciate.

Amazingly, my mother has been living with her one lung now for twenty-one years. When she recovered from her surgery, she told me to get out and live my life. Mother had always waited…until the kids were grown…until her mother passed on…until the house was paid for. Then, she got cancer.

I took my mother's advice and began a new journey. I had been working as Director of Special Events and Assistant Director of Group Sales for the Louisville Redbirds AAA baseball team and the Louisville River Frogs ECHL hockey team. I took a promotion that moved me to small-town Texas. I was Marketing Director of the Central Texas Stampede, one of the charter teams in the Western Professional Hockey League—one of the leagues that took hockey to the South and later merged with the Central Hockey League. That job was a nightmare that ended in my termination and a four-year lawsuit to collect my salary and commissions. I was let go just before the hockey seasons began, so I was essentially unemployable in my industry.

I worked as a temporary secretary for approximately one year before

I found work even remotely related to my experience. I padded that income by working in a department store. At times I wondered why I got my degree, and longed for the days at UPS. Then, I got a job at Cortland College in the State University of New York (SUNY) system. It wasn't exactly what I had hoped for, but I was managing an ice arena again and was surrounded by academia. As my lawsuit against the Stampede continued, my interest in the law increased. I took a Business Law class at night and decided to pursue my law degree.

Since I was the first in my immediate family to pursue a law or advanced degree, I had no idea how to go about it. I started at the University of Pittsburgh, relying on the school's assurance that I would only have to pay out-of-state tuition for a year. Although first-year students are prohibited from working while enrolled in classes, I had no choice. I babysat, waited tables at a private club for the very wealthy and interned for a blind attorney. When I discovered the school's misrepresentations, I transferred back to SUNY's University at Buffalo, where I knew no one.

In law school, the bonds are formed in the first year when the students travel in sections and attend the same classes with the same people. I had to leave that security and try to infiltrate a similar system in a new school. It reminded me of childhood, when I had transferred to the public school downtown because my dad stopped paying child support and my mother couldn't afford to keep me and my two sisters in the school near our home. Still, I kept my eyes on the prize in law school—as I always have. I knew I was there for the education above all else. Even when one instructor told me I "lived in la-la land" and would probably never see my law license, I pressed on.

My lawsuit went to trial while I was in law school. I obtained a default judgment that I will never collect on. However, I learned tons about the law and the stress of being a litigant. I keep that in mind as I defend cases and advise clients today. It wasn't a complete loss; although I am not sure I would ever opt to have my life put on hold and scrutinized so heavily that way again. It was almost as traumatic an experience as the abuse I took on the job before I was terminated.

Contrary to the views of some professors and administrators who devalued me during law school, I graduated and then passed the bar within months following graduation. I had my first interview in the New York City area at 9 a.m. on September 11, 2001. I was forever connected to NYC and its people that day. I decided that regardless of whether I got the job, I would return to volunteer. I got the job, stayed a few months, and got my "springboard job" soon after.

In my first job as a licensed attorney, I was hired on a Thursday as an associate in the workers' compensation department. On Friday, the managing attorney resigned. By the following Tuesday, I found myself managing the department. Four months later, I was trying cases in the State Supreme Court. It sounds so cliché, but failure really wasn't an option. I worked night and day learning the law and procedure while managing the existing caseload with my limited knowledge. I didn't want anyone to know how inexperienced I was, so I did all I could to reach the level of competence of my competitors. My efforts apparently paid off, but it wasn't enough to salvage the firm that is now defunct.

I was reluctant to risk sole proprietorship so early in my career, but my clients, mentors and co-workers encouraged it. On June 23, 2003, I opened a home- based firm with one case. By the end of the month, I was managing approximately 30 cases. By the end of the year, there were close to 100 cases, and I appeared in civil court on negligence cases up to five times per week for former colleagues and opponents who had scheduling conflicts. Currently, I manage up to 200 cases for a major insurance carrier, a national third-party administrator and several corporations. I also provide business and conflict resolution counseling to businesses of all sizes. I am focusing on my law practice and enjoying my new lease on life. I have two wonderful families: the one I was born with and the one I have chosen in my friends. I am now learning to enjoy the beauty in each day and live a life of gratitude, rather than self-punishment.

My hero growing up was my mother, without a doubt. In early 1970s Louisville, she had the courage to do what many women now do without thinking because of strong women like her. I didn't understand how special her sacrifices were until much later in life. I was only about 18 months old when she decided she would not raise her daughters in the environment we were experiencing. After the police came to the door in the middle of the night, she had enough. She told herself each day that tomorrow would be better, and sometimes it was. Sometimes my dad wouldn't drink as much. Sometimes he was very sweet. Sometimes he would actually help out a little. But the embezzlement was the last straw.

Mother had tried to follow the rules of the Catholic Church. Our family was so Catholic that several of our cousins were priests and nuns. My dad donated time and money to the church, so everyone thought he was such a great man. But he was a terrible dad and a worse husband. She kicked him out and decided to give us the most stable environment she could. She had no idea at the time how much debt she would be left with and how little money to live on.

Our church leaders did almost nothing to help us keep food and shelter. They did everything they could to punish all of us for what they deemed as her sin in divorcing. Or at least that's the way it seemed to me. I couldn't understand why a church would teach love, yet be so unloving. Yet my mom kept us in church and gave us the foundation of faith. We struggled to keep even the basics, but she taught us all to contribute. And that is how we not only survived, but excelled.

When my mom battled cancer three times and won, she solidified her place as my lifelong hero. Her values and all the work she did to give them to me those early years continue to be my foundation and have helped me build the solid life she wanted for me.

For the young girls seeking their voices today, start by listening and observing. Listen to those you admire, and observe their behavior. Do they do as they say you should? Are they rude or cruel to anyone? If their words and their actions are not consistent in all environments, you probably aren't seeing them as they truly are. Withhold your trust from them. If they put their needs before yours and dismiss yours when you assert them, walk away. They are not your friends. They will hurt you, sometimes unintentionally. You are here to live, love and enjoy life. If you are not, take one new action today and another each day until you are living, loving and enjoying your life more than not.

I know you have doubts. I know you will doubt yourself. You will have moments where you think you deserve punishment and cruelty. You do not. I have been abused by a family member. I have been raped, as a child and as an adult. I have hated myself. I have hated my life. I even tried to take it. I have since learned that my life is mine to create, with whatever tools I have at any given moment. The most important tool I have now is my mind—the ability to reprogram it, to tune out the messages I don't want and to create a view of the world as beautiful, full of love and unlimited. I choose how I want to see the world by choosing where I want to focus, and I finally focus more on the gifts: sunshine, freedom, a smile, a good night's sleep, play, a job well done, etc., rather than on the work that still needs to be done. As Gandhi said, you must "be the change you wish to see in the world." It starts with your mind and what you do daily.

PAULETTE ROBINSON

PAULETTE ROBINSON IS AN ACCOMPLISHED wedding and event planner with over 10 years of extensive experience and training in all areas of bridal consulting, wedding and event planning and coordination.

In 1994 Ms. Robinson earned her bachelor's degree in Business Management and a secondary degree in Entrepreneurship. She began her career in customer service and soon moved into project management. As a senior level Project Manager within several corporations including Scholastic, Inc., the largest publisher of children's books, Ms. Robinson sharpened her organization, people management and coordination skills. Her experience and accomplishments including the development, management and successful launch of Scholastic's two online commerce stores made the decision to follow her dream of full-time wedding and event planning and coordination an easy transition.

Formally a member of the Association of Bridal Consultants, Ms. Robinson continues to hone her skills and stay abreast of the latest industry trends and etiquette, teaching at a local community college in New Jersey to share that knowledge. Additionally, she has sat under the tutelage of many top industry professionals including Colin Cowie and David Tutera (wedding planner for Star Jones).

In 2006 Ms. Robinson made her television debut on "Whose Wedding Is It Anyway?" the Style Network's highly acclaimed wedding show. Her appearance was met with much enthusiasm and she has since participated in two additional episodes of the show, and one episode of their spin-off destination show, Married Away. Additionally, she served as an expert panelist on HGTV's Ultimate Wedding Guide special which aired in June 2007.

Overall, Ms. Robinson is known for her ability to plan, host, and organize some of the most unforgettable weddings and events ever produced from small intimate settings in Old San Juan, Puerto Rico, to large weekend- long events in Las Vegas, Nevada.

I was the youngest of seven children, and reaped the benefits of parents who had perfected the formula for raising grounded children. It began with a firm foundation: an introduction to God. Never forceful but always consistent, my parents made sure that knowledge and understanding of God and Christ were central to our upbringing. Sunday school and church were a given.

Their greatest success in this area was that they lived the values they encouraged in us. They didn't force anything that they themselves did not truly believe and actually live. I can honestly say that my parents were the same in and out of the home. That taught me truth and integrity.

My mother, Doris Robinson, had the most influence on my upbringing since my father drove a tractor-trailer and spent much of his time on the road being the provider that I grew up knowing, loving and admiring.

My mother's paramount parenting skill was raising each of us (especially me) based on our individual strengths and weaknesses. She made sure we were very honest with ourselves about our strengths and weaknesses then she encouraged and honed them individually. My mother recognized that I was a born leader, and was also aware that left unchecked, this gift could easily become a tool of manipulation. Thus, she made me keenly aware of the fact that she could not be manipulated, but could be a good follower of an honest leader. That coupled with my faith in God has always been where I draw my energy, strength and courage from.

As an immigrant from Panama, my mother made her foray into the land of employment at a Woolworth's store in New York. She explained that nervous (but determined) she made her way to the department store on a chilly December afternoon. After completing the mandatory math exam and paperwork she was escorted to meet the hiring manager. Unlike most interviews, where the manager sits behind a desk and engages in Q & A, because it was holiday season this manager was on the sales floor unloading a delivery of poinsettias. The manager and my mother began to talk as he grabbed one plant after the next off the delivery cart and set it on the display shelf. My mother immediately began to help and converse and needless to say this natural initiative landed her first job in the United States.

It sounds so cliché but my mother was and will always be my one and only hero. I remember participating in a pageant during college. At the question and answer section I was asked who my female heroine was. I stopped, thought, and tried to run through my mind stories of all the great women I'd heard of...but in those few quick moments I could only say what was natural and sincere: "Doris Robinson." Years later I wondered if that answer was based on a lack of knowledge or creativity...and I could ask the same thing about naming her now. But in reality she is indeed my hero, and I now fully know and understand why.

When I was growing up one of the first observations I made about my mother as a mother was her incredible ability to anticipate a need and then meet it before you had to ask or explain. From simple things like having the necessities for your class trip laid out on your bed when you returned home, to larger more important things like the car I so desperately needed my third year of college to be able to get to two jobs and classes. As a growing adult I began to understand that her ability was born from the gift of being able to think beyond yourself in order to consider others. Now anyone would say, "Well, yeah, that's what mothers are supposed to do" but my mother did this for anyone she came into contact with. Sometimes just the simple expression of her wisdom shed the much needed light on a situation that someone had been toiling with.

She's my hero because I watched breast cancer turn a buxom, healthy woman with smooth chocolate skin to a thin, sometimes frail, giant whose spirit and courage were never shaken or ravaged by the disease. In the two months before my mother passed away from cancer we traveled together to a women's conference where my mother was the study leader. During that event she spoke openly and honestly about her cancer and then said she had spoken very bluntly to God about how this would end and when. She said she was not at liberty to share His response but that she was at was peace with who she was and how much He loved her.

My mother is my hero because she understood that truth in the face of any adversity wins always. Although I grew up hearing stories of distant great women warriors and social changers, I had the opportunity to live with, watch and experience all that made Doris Robinson a hero.

To young women trying to find their voice, I echo my mother's words: "Play by yourself." Growing up my mother taught me this lesson. I always wanted to visit a friend or have a friend over, and for the most part I was able to. But on some occasions my mother would say, "No...learn to play by yourself." Then she would launch into this soliloquy of how important it was...blah, blah, blah which is what it sounded like to me as a five-year- old. But as I began to grow and recite the speech in my head it all became clear. She was teaching me how to listen to my own voice, to become familiar and comfortable with who I am as a person.

"Learn to play by yourself," she would say. "You have to learn and decide who you are and what you stand for before you allow every and anyone to influence your thoughts and your convictions. If you're always surrounded by people, you begin to shape your thoughts around what is acceptable by the group and the thoughts are no longer (or never) original. It becomes a group effort and you're just one of the muddled contributors who have bought into an idea that you may not at your core really agree with. It's just easier to follow the crowd so you put your thoughts to the side and concede to the group thought. What do you think? You'll never know if you don't develop and get to know yourself before you let everyone else define you. Play by yourself."

Later when I was introduced to the notion of co- dependency I closed my eyes and thanked God for my mother and that I learned to play by myself. I've never struggled with the need to be validated by other people or situations. I learned to walk through life doing what was and is comfortable for me and what I believe and know is the next step in my progression. I never stopped to get multiple opinions from the group, who might discourage me right out of my blessing. Instead, I always consult God and then proceed with His great blessings.

Girls, play by yourself sometimes. Travel by yourself, go to dinner by yourself, and take in a movie, play or concert by yourself. Get to know who and what you're capable of by yourself. Trust me, when you're by yourself you can hear your own voice...it's never lost, you just have to listen.

SANDY STEIN

M Y HERO GROWING UP WAS my dad. He had me and my sister late in life, but always kept up with all the other dads, even surpassing them in fun events. He always told me that I could be whoever and whatever I wanted to be, and when I decided to be a stewardess (in the '70s that is what we were called), though he had hoped that I would go to college and be a professional, he totally (well mostly) accepted my decision, especially because I said it was going to be for just a year. It was actually thirty-five years.

My dad was a dentist, and in his 60s while I was still a teenager, he lost his practice. Not only did he not give up, but he figured out a better way to make a living utilizing the skills that he already had. I watched and learned.

My son Alex was ten when my husband announced that he no longer wanted to work. I was fifty-three and a part time flight attendant who knew I could not provide for my son with the little amount of income that I was bringing in.

That night, needless to say, I was TICKED OFF! I couldn't believe that my husband could be so selfish. So I prayed to my dad in heaven, asking for some guidance. Though it sounds crazy, my dad came to me in a dream and gave me the idea to create a new product that would prevent keys from falling to the bottom of my purse.

I awoke the following morning, and remembered the dream vividly. I fashioned a prototype of the idea, and it was just like I remembered it in the dream. I took one very long look at the item, and knew it was my destiny to get it into the market place, but first it needed a name. Since it found keys in your purse I called it Finders Key Purse® (like finders keepers, losers weepers). When heaven talks you better listen!

Again, my dad made a huge difference in my choosing my career paths. I never thought of becoming a flight attendant, but I did, and along the way I learned a lot about life. In my second career as inventor and business owner, not only did my dad give me the idea of the invention through a dream, but when it came for me to put a business together with no college or formal business education, I remembered how my dad utilized the skills that he had learned as a dentist to find his next career in his 60s. I did just that.

I drew from life experiences as a flight attendant and went forward, even though there were many naysayers. If it worked for my Dad, I figured I had a good shot at it too. Sometimes your "ah ha" moment comes from just one thing that your mentor said or did that really made a difference in how you perceive going forward. It is true for me: "Necessity WAS the Mother of Invention"!

Alex has been working with me for the past few years as my Warehouse Manager while going to school to become a criminologist—he says there will always be criminals so his job will always be secure.

———◆———

The most important words of encouragement that I could give anyone is to tell them that they are not their title. Along life's path we get labeled—smart, sly, slow, a stewardess, a drop out. No matter what "title" you are given, forget it, and realize that who you really are is not always visible on the outside. Concentrate on what makes you feel good and powerful, and you will see the miracles that result!

TERESA ALEXANDER

KIDS ACHIEVING FINANCIAL SUCCESS (KAFS) came about as the product of Teresa's hard-earned lessons. This nonprofit organization educates lower income children ages nine to 18 about earning, saving and investing their money. Through a series of workshops, students are made to understand the concept of money and credit by applying it to their everyday lives.

As Director of KAFS, Alexander teaches students that credit is like their GPA. Just like grades, credit status is looked at closely. It is based upon the students' means to pay back their debts with the resources they have. And if they don't have enough resources available, they have to come up with another solution. It is then that we get onto the topic of how to generate and budget money. An important distinction is made between wants versus needs—what the kids need in their lives rather than what they simply want. After a series of these workshops, they apply the skills they have learned to create fund-raisers.

For two years now, KAFS has held student-planned fund-raisers to give children hands-on experience making money. The youngsters manage community- wide car washes, fashion shows and golf tournaments, among other events. "My dream is for KAFS to be a fun financial experience as well as educational," says Alexander.

With their fund-raising earnings, students create individual portfolios. They are taught ways to manage this "capital" until they are 18 and able to collect it in the form of college tuition, stocks, bonds or even down payments toward their first homes. KAFS graduates come out of their experience not only with an investment portfolio and a bank account, but also with lifelong lessons that keep paying off. They continue to reinvest the money that originated from that very first car wash.

Alexander is thrilled with the progress of her organization and expects enrollment in KAFS to double this year. She continues to work tirelessly on behalf of these kids and hopes to expand her facilities once she garners additional support. For Alexander, it's all about changing children's financial futures, one workshop at a time. Learn more about KAFS at kafsfoundation.org.

———◆———

My name is Teresa Alexander. I was born and raised in Sacramento, California. In 1966, my parents moved from Waco, Texas to start a family life in Sacramento, CA where both parents worked as factory workers. My parents divorced and my mother was left to raise seven children. My mother has always worked two jobs to support the family. She believed in providing for her children.

I recall a time in high school when my mother and I shared everything from the clothes that she purchased to the only car that we drove. I was responsible for making sure my siblings made it to school on time and food was prepared when they returned home. However, as I got older and wanted to help my mother out financially, I took on a job at Taco Bell while attending high school. The job allowed me to open an account and start saving for the things that I really wanted. I recall being introduced to credit cards and received a card from every retail store and bank that I could. I was not aware of the financial dangers of credit until I lost my job. One payment after another had come in mail for me to pay. I panicked because I was afraid of the possibilities of what could happen according to the bill collectors. The bill collectors did not offer any solution to the debt problem that I was having. I was continuously harassed until I changed my phone number and found no way out. I ran from the problem in hopes that it would resolve itself. However, a few years later I enrolled into college, started a family and wanted to purchase my first home.

I tried to make a big purchase and low and behold my past was still there. I was faced with an enormous amount of debt. I contacted the creditor and was informed that the debt needed to be paid in order to make any purchase and establish my credit again. I created a list of creditors and paid each one off one by one. Although the creditors received payment my credit was not in good shape because I had defaulted on the original agreement with the retail stores. I was able to make my first home purchase but the interest rate that I received was extremely high. I realized at that point that I needed to share my story with others before it was too late.

I started networking with other families and came up with different themes that we could discuss and make it work to keep the kids' interest while educating them at the same time. This is how I started Kids Achieving Financial Success. The program offers an array of classes that teach kids from the age of nine to 18 the importance of financial literacy. The classes are conducted once a week and taught by financial experts from the community. The children gain knowledge through hands-on experience, and by the end of the program the members receive financial portfolios that include a savings account. The program has been in existence since 2007 and continues to arm our children with the financial savvy that it will take to be productive citizens.

Growing up my hero was Mary McLeod Bethune. She paved the way for others to make a way when nothing else existed. I admire people who, regardless of their circumstances, can find a way to make the world a better place.

Oprah Winfrey has also been an inspiration in my life. I have watched her over the years develop into the person she is today. She has lived the struggle and continues to be part of the solution. I admire her sharing her hard work over the years.

For young girls currently seeking their voices: Don't be afraid to do you! If you can dream it, believe it and it will be done. Know that circumstances are only temporary. You must take a stance for what you believe and GO FOR IT!

teresal_alexander@yahoo.com
916-682-2405
916-714-5236

THE MISSION OF THIS BOOK

OUR PASSION IS HELPING YOUNG women find a place in life, especially those young women needing support and encouragement when entering the big, wide world. We wish to assist girls who come of age in foster care or group homes and must try to find their own paths to success.

Therefore, we want the proceeds of our book to help us open a home to aid girls in transition—girls whose upbringing may have lacked opportunity for growth and/or family support. We hope to help these girls realize and nurture their talents, potentials, and gifts of spirit.

N.U.S.W. is all about empowerment. How fortunate are we that the remarkable women in our book share their knowledge, spirit, and incredible strength through their personal experiences and by giving young girls the words of wisdom and heroic inspirations that have helped them along the way!

We thought it important during this time of great idealism, while adolescent girls are actively searching for meaning, that we keep the safety net up and respect their uniqueness and encourage their growth into productive adults.

N.U.S.W. is one of those nets.

—Joyce and Kerin

Please visit our website at
www.nustrengthofwomen.com

CPSIA information can be obtained
at www.ICGtesting.com
Printed in the USA
BVOW09s2114061017
496925BV00001B/2/P